THE SOUL OF SAMUEL PEPYS

BY

GAMALIEL BRADFORD

Author of "Damaged Souls," "American Portraits"
"Lee the American," etc.

WITH ILLUSTRATIONS

BOSTON AND NEW YORK

HOUGHTON MIFFLIN COMPANY

The Riverside Press Cambridge

1924

The Riverside Press
CAMBRIDGE · MASSACHUSETTS
PRINTED IN THE U.S.A.

TO

ALFRED C. POTTER

WHO FOR THIRTY YEARS

HAS SHARED MY WONDER AT THE GREAT DIARY

AND MY AFFECTION FOR ITS AUTHOR

*We care most for those portraits in which
we find ourselves.*

VOLTAIRE

PREFACE

SOME apology may seem to be required for an attempt to portray the soul of one who has painted his own portrait with such ample and intimate fidelity. That portrait has been studied with delight by generations of readers and has won the enthusiastic praise of critics so varied as Scott and Thackeray and Lowell and Stevenson, to name no others. Nevertheless, the very amplitude of the great Diary makes it difficult for the hurried reader to approach. It has the abundance, the crowded, formless richness, the embarrassing complication of an actual lived life. And it seemed as if it might be possible to introduce a certain amount of order and clarity into the shapeless mass, so as to make it more available for those who have not the patience to deal with it in its tangled entirety. As with all my portraits, I have endeavoured to let the subject speak for himself, simply adding such comment of my own or of others as may make the utterance more effective. But never before have I had material so splendid or so inexhaustible. I have lived with the Diary intimately for thirty years; but only when I came to work on it for psychographic purposes did I fully appreciate its incomparable value as a human document.

The bibliography of Pepys's record is exceedingly interesting, but too complicated for discussion here. The Diary was first deciphered from the original difficult shorthand by the Reverend John Smith and a portion of it published by Lord Braybrooke in 1825. Various editions, containing more and more material, followed throughout the nineteenth century, until Mr. H. B. Wheatley issued what is probably the final one, containing all that it is decently possible to print.

Of the numerous books and essays about Pepys the more important are Mr. Wheatley's "Samuel Pepys and the World He Lived In" and Mr. Moorhouse's "Samuel Pepys, Administrator, Observer, Gossip." Among very recent writings I have found much that was helpful in Mr. Ponsonby's discussion of "English Diaries," with its suggestive analysis of the various motives of diary-writing. I may also mention the careful study of Admiral Sir William Penn by my daughter, Sarah Rice Bradford.

On the difficult subject of the pronunciation of Pepys's name I need not enlarge further than to quote Mr. Wheatley: "At present there are three pronunciations in use — *Peps*, which is the most usual; *Peeps*, which is the received one at Magdalene College, and

PREFACE

Peppis, which I learn from Mr. Walter C. Pepys is the one used by other branches of the family." I myself have become habituated to *Peeps*, which is said to be still used by the descendants of Pepys's sister, Paulina. But *Peps* will probably always obtain most widely. The best comment on the whole matter is Sterne's description of the three roads from Calais to Paris: "First, the road by Lisle and Arras, which is the most about — but most interesting and instructing. The second, that by Amiens, which you may go if you would see Chantilly. And that by Beauvais, which you may go if you will. For this reason a great many choose to go by Beauvais."

In the quotations from the Diary I have endeavored to reproduce exactly the spelling and capitals of the text as given by Mr. Wheatley. In all other quotations I have followed my usual practice of modernizing and standardizing in every respect: if it were possible in all cases to print from a writer's original manuscript, it might be worth while to attempt to imitate his typographical vagaries; but I see no reason for considering the whims of unreliable editors.

GAMALIEL BRADFORD

WELLESLEY HILLS, MASSACHUSETTS.

CONTENTS

ILLUSTRATIONS

CHRONOLOGY

Samuel Pepys, born (place uncertain), February 23, 1633.

Educated at Huntingdon and at St. Paul's School, London, till 1650.

Graduated B.A. at Cambridge, 1653.

Married Elizabeth St. Michel, December 1, 1655.

Operation for stone, March 26, 1658.

Became a clerk of the Exchequer, 1659.

Diary begins, January 1, 1660.

Went to Holland with Montagu to fetch the king, spring of 1660.

Became Clerk of the Acts, July, 1660.

Defended the Naval Administration at the Bar of the House of Commons, March 5, 1668.

Diary ends, May 31, 1669.

Wife died, November 10, 1669.

Became Secretary for the Affairs of the Navy, 1673.

Elected to Parliament, November, 1673.

Sent to Tower in connection with the Popish Plot, 1679.

Accompanied Lord Dartmouth to Tangier, 1683.

Became Secretary of the Admiralty, 1684.

Died, May 26, 1703.

THE SOUL OF
SAMUEL PEPYS

I

THE MAN AND THE DIARY

I

SAMUEL PEPYS was twenty-seven years old in 1660
when the Stuarts were restored to the throne of
England, in the person of King Charles the Second.
Therefore the prime of Pepys's life was passed during
the Restoration period, and it is essential to understand that period as forming the background to his
character.

It was an abnormal age, an age of turbulence and
reaction, a backwater in the stream of English and
human progress. From 1640 to 1660 the stern Puritan
strain was dominant, typifying itself in the iron figure
of Cromwell, striving to mould and force the human
spirit into strict bands of conventional virtue, aiming
at a high ideal, but aiming at it by harsh and artificial methods such as sooner or later drive the average
man into hypocrisy and rebellion.

No doubt there was plenty of hypocrisy in England
first, and then came the open rebellion. The average

I

man stirred in his troubled dream, roused himself, rubbed his eyes, threw off the unnatural yoke, and with a sigh turned back to the pleasant, comfortable, easy-going life of this world, which he instinctively felt would be best sustained and fostered by a Stuart régime.

And of course the tradition of twenty years was not abolished so speedily. The survival of older elements and their blending with newer, both fundamentally human, and artificially imported, make a strange, seething conglomerate, which, if neither normal nor worthy of permanence, is most curious and fascinating to study and analyze. There was the past Puritan world, lingering in quiet corners, always ready to assert itself in sullen protest against immoral innovation, a world best personified perhaps in the grand, remote, ideal figure of the old blind Milton. There was the Cromwellian army, scattered through the land in peaceable pursuits, but saturated with undying memories of its heroic leader. There was the horde and swarm of new political ambitions, such as always infest a changing government, men who had little to lose by instability and everything to gain, men of quick tongue, ready intellect, and pliable conscience, eager to worm themselves into the indolent confidence of the half-foreign king. There were the caterers to public amusement, poets, dramatists, men of letters, madly anxious to bring the world back to the enjoyment of artistic beauty, but far more thoughtful and conscious of the form of their productions and of their immediate effect than of the profound basis of human truth. There was the great body of the English people, essentially sound and conservative in their instincts, but weary of the strain of a formal virtue pitched too high, and longing to taste something of the sweet of life, which for a generation had been denied them. And at the top and in the forefront of this mixed scene was a thoroughly artificial court, aping, as far as it could, the habits and manners of France, flaunting a bravado of careless immorality in the face of defeated Puritanism, seeking the pleasure of the hour, regardless of the future, regardless of the greatness of England.

Into this complicated, ardent, and in many respects corrupting world was thrust the soul of Samuel Pepys, with a wholesome instinct of self-preservation and a keen desire for enjoyment. His natural position in life might be called medium, or something above. He was fairly well born, fairly well educated, and had excellent connections. But he was anything but wealthy, and having married very young, he had to battle for pleasure and even for comfort. As he was average in station, so he may be said on the whole to have been average in character; below the average in some points, perhaps, decidedly above it in others, but on the whole distinctly representative.

He had the average practical instincts of life, could do a day's work, groan over it and rebel against it, but do it. He could drive a hard bargain, and then, when his sympathy or vanity was touched, give away a round sum, or throw it away. He had an average intelligence, could apply keen analysis to a problem that affected his own interest, made mistakes, imbibed prejudices, misjudged men and life and God and paid for it. Take him all in all, and allowing for his surroundings, he was average in morals, indulged his passions and regretted the indulgence, made good resolutions and broke them and made them again, judged others severely and himself leniently and severely also, fought the old mad battle with the flesh and the devil, sometimes shamefully, sometimes triumphantly, but always humanly. In short, he was a man amazingly like you and me, and the chief among all the many interests of his wonderful Diary is that it reveals him and you and me with a candor, an unparalleled, direct, sincere clarity, which has never been equaled, except perhaps in the Essays of Montaigne. If he was average in the essentials of his

4

character, his power of displaying that character and
his frankness in doing so were not average at all.

We have to begin, however, by viewing the man's
life externally, as it might appear to us if the Diary
had never existed. And first to consider his public life
and its larger relations with the world. During the
fifties Pepys acted as business agent to his kinsman,
Lord Sandwich, and filled a minor position in connection with the Exchequer. Shortly after the
Restoration, he became connected with the Navy in
the important office of Clerk of the Acts, and from
this time on his public life was mainly bound up with
naval affairs. He was zealous, faithful, and intelligent
in the performance of his duties and earned the respect
and commendation of his equals and superiors. He
continued these naval activities, first as Clerk of the
Acts and then as Secretary for Naval Affairs and of the
Admiralty, with certain interruptions and intervals,
till the Revolution of 1688. His marine experience, if
one may venture the contradiction, was mainly confined to the land, though in 1683 he was member of an
expedition to Tangier, as to which he kept a Journal
of historical interest,[1] but without the vividness of the
earlier Diary. Business capacity on land is perhaps
quite as essential to naval success as sailorship at sea,
and in this limited function Pepys evidently deserves

all sorts of credit. "The ablest man in the English Admiralty," [2] says Macaulay, and I do not know that any one need say more, though Pepys's most recent biographer, Mr. Morehouse, enlarging upon the Secretary's later efforts, declares that "the Diarist sinks into insignificance beside the official who did more than any single man to reform the administration of the Navy." [3] If we wish to add the testimony of a contemporary, there is that of Lord Berkeley, who wrote to Pepys himself: "It would be very difficult for His Majesty to find a successor so qualified in all respects for his service, if we consider both your integrity, vast abilities, industry, and zealous affection for his service." [4]

Pepys's public life, outside of his naval duties, is of less importance. He was a member of Parliament, useful no doubt, but not especially conspicuous. Owing to the religious connections of his wife and to his own intimate relation with the Duke of York, as head of the Navy, he was more or less entangled in the vast web of the Popish Plot, and was at one time imprisoned in the Tower; and he was involved in some other complications such as necessarily beset a public man in those hazardous days. But he came out of all with his credit intact, and after the Revolution, which naturally cut him off from political activity, he lived to enjoy a comfortable old age, dying on the 26th of May, 1703.

Of Pepys's private life we know comparatively little, independent of the Diary; at least it seems little, since the Diary-years, from 1660 to 1669, are lit with such a glare of intimate familiarity and comprehension. Many of the letters of his later period have been pre-served, and they somewhat amplify the knowledge derived from the Diary, without suggesting anything seriously incompatible with it. But they are formal and conventional compared to the more personal record. Pepys's boyhood was passed partly in the country and partly in London. He was educated at Saint Paul's School and then at Cambridge. The chief fact definitely known as to his university career is that he was admonished for being drunk.[5] But his later life conclusively proves that he made fair use of his educational opportunities. He admits that he was favorable to the Puritan régime;[6] yet it is safe to as-sume that his enthusiasm was tempered with cau-tion. In 1655, when he was twenty-two, he married Elizabeth St. Michel, a girl of fifteen, of Catholic connections, and with no money, but with the good looks that always had a fascination for her susceptible husband. They lived through the rubs and strains of poverty together to moderate affluence; but Mrs.

7

THE SOUL OF SAMUEL PEPYS

Pepys died in 1669, just beyond the limit of the Diary period, immediately after their return from a brief and apparently delightful trip abroad. They had no children, and Pepys's family interest was bestowed upon his brothers and sister and their offspring and also to a moderate extent upon the relatives of his wife. He never married again, but continued a decent bachelor existence, having always an orderly, if not luxurious, establishment in which to entertain the numerous friends who were glad to come to him. He had intellectual tastes and was able to indulge them, liked the theatre, adored music and was proficient in it, read widely and collected books with passion, leaving a library of great interest and value to Magdalene College, Cambridge, where it is preserved to this day.

In short, if we read his career in the records of others, we must set him down as a most respectable and respected citizen, who lived a long life of profit and usefulness and died esteemed and moderately regretted by many persons whose esteem was as well worth having as that of any in his time. As to his standing in this world we cannot have better testimony than that of the admirable John Evelyn, in his Diary: "He was universally beloved, hospitable, generous, learned in many things, skilled in music, a very great cherisher of learned men of whom he had the

MRS. PEPYS AS ST. KATHARINE

conversation." [7] As to his prospects in the other the Reverend George Hickes bears witness in impressive fashion: "The greatness of his behaviour in his long and sharp trial before his death, was in every respect answerable to his great life; and I believe no man ever went out of this world with greater contempt of it, or a more lively faith in every thing that was revealed of the world to come. . . . I never attended any sick or dying person that died with so much Christian greatness of mind, or a more lively sense of immortality, or so much fortitude and patience in so long and sharp a trial, or greater resignation to what he most devoutly acknowledged to be the wisdom of God." [8]

II

But he kept a diary and showed the lining of his soul as well as the costly furred and trimmed exterior, and some persons have been puzzled and perplexed by the contrast. The diary-instinct is rather curious, at any rate in its extreme manifestations. It takes an amazing patience, and fidelity, and assiduity, to sit down day after day and narrate the day's doings and experiences, often at considerable length. You come in late and tired and dragged and sleepy. Bed seems the only thing worth while. Yet, if you have the diary-instinct, you get out the well-worn book and note down much

9

or little, before you are contented to go to rest. Look at the forty years' persistence of Greville, or of Edmond de Goncourt. Then there was John Quincy Adams. The printed diary, kept during more than fifty years, fills twelve closely printed volumes of five hundred pages each, and there is half as much again unprinted. Think of the dogged, intense perseverance required to maintain such a habit through health and sickness and happiness and unhappiness, till the very end.

And immediately one begins to speculate as to the motives that may inspire this remarkable procedure. No doubt they are complicated, like the motives of most action. First, there is the plain instinct of record. Nations like to keep their systematic annals. The diary is the annals of the individual, to which he and those who come after him can turn for the dated, indisputable facts of current daily life. The immense utility of the practice, from this point of view, has been sufficiently demonstrated. An interesting modification of it is the diary as a literary or scientific notebook, in which writers like Emerson or Thoreau or scores of others jot down impressions and observations which can be worked up afterwards into more elaborate and finished form.

Also, there arises the question how far do diarists

generally think of future publication, how far do they have more or less vaguely in mind the possibility of blazing out to distant posterity with the fame of a Saint-Simon or a Greville or an Amiel? With the brief daily pencilled jotting that you and I make hastily this question does not exist. But I believe that all the more elaborate keepers of journals * have had something of the kind obscurely before them. Some admit it openly. The Goncourts refer to future publication and evidently have it in mind on all occasions. The delightful diary of Thomas Moore was confessedly written that it might serve as a source of income to the poet's wife after his death. And this vivid consciousness of the future reader must to a certain extent affect the candor and spontaneity of the diarist. He will express himself differently when he is thinking of the curious eye of another human being from what he would do if he were soliloquizing for his own soul and God. Yet I suspect that the shyest and most personal of diarists does not wholly escape this preoccupation and is inclined to shape his sentences with as much grace and finish as possible, in view of posterity's ap-

---

* The terms "journal" and "diary" seem to be almost interchangeable; but "journal" should probably be used for a more elaborate record. Mr. Arthur Ponsonby, in his excellent book on "English Diaries," suggests that "journals" are more external than "diaries"; but this distinction is certainly not observed.

proval and applause. Amiel dissected his own soul with as little attitude as any man. Yet even Amiel said, "Leave the legacy of your own heart and thought: you can do nothing more useful to mankind." [9]

Probably, however, in most cases of diary-keeping the motive is obscure to the diarist himself, and what fundamentally holds him to his daily task is the curious instinct of self-expression which so overpoweringly and constantly impels us to find escape somehow, anyhow, from the close, tormenting prison of our own microscopic, infinite selves. The more natural form of this instinct is the openly, directly social. We seek immediately and by word of mouth to establish the intimate contact of soul with soul which, alas, can never be established in this isolating world. And it will be found, I think, that the elaborate diarist generally is one who is less inclined to, less successful with, this immediate social contact. He is shy, secretive, introspective, often eremitical, and precisely because he shrinks from laying bare his spiritual secrets to the prying gaze of the flesh and blood about him, he is all the more disposed to reveal his heart in those private pages which he comes to love as if they represented the most intimate possibilities of friendship.

But, whatever the motive of diary-keeping, there is

no doubt about its immense value to all those who are curious as to the profounder depths of human nature. As one who has made a life-work of probing those depths, if only for a little way, I can say that nothing has had so much importance or significance for me as diaries. And let it not be thought that the interest of such study is a mere impertinent and gossiping curiosity. What gives it at once immortal worth and also a certain sacredness is the tremendous identity of human hearts, the fact that when the diarist records his inmost secrets he is recording your secrets and my secrets as well as his own. Not, of course, that all hearts are exactly alike. The differences are as interesting as the resemblances. But the differences are interesting because of the resemblances, and nothing comes nearer to satisfying that eternal craving to escape from ourselves than the ever-renewed realization of how much there is in the experiences and passions and hopes of others that is precisely identical with our own. All books teach us this in some degree, especially the revelations of the great novelists and poets. But for those who know how to read, it is taught most in personal literature, that is, letters, and even more in the special form with which we are now occupied, the diary or journal.

Without attempting any pedantic bibliography of

the vast field of diary-literature, it will be of interest, preliminary to the study of Pepys, to review briefly the main different types of such literature, and so to appreciate how vast the field is and how great its fascination.

To begin with, there is the diary that is sincere and the diary that is not, the diary that springs *almost* unconsciously from the depths of the writer's spirit and that which is written at all times with some thought of the effect it may produce upon a possible or probable reader. No such sharp line can perhaps be drawn in practice; but there are extremes in either kind which are distinctly illustrative. At one extreme stands Pepys. At the other, I think, stands the Diary of Madame D'Arblay. Not that Fanny Burney meant to deceive. On the contrary, she would have been almost painfully averse to anything like a conscious falsehood. It is simply that she is always posing before a spiritual mirror and every word is instinctively adapted to convey some special impression, quite apart from the direct, immediate portrayal of the diarist's actual experience. Take another diary of essentially artificial quality, that of Grant Duff. Here was a man with magnificent opportunities for making a historical record; but he indicates in his epigraph that he will be careful to set down nothing but what is agreeable, and I ask you, how can a man keep a diary of any consequence on such a principle as that? Again, among the diaries of lesser interest there is that of Joseph Farington, recently printed, which, in the natural enthusiasm of discovery, has been greatly over-rated as well as lamentably over-edited. Here also was a man with admirable opportunities, with which he could not fail to tell much that was interesting. And he was obviously sincere enough. But his record is jejune and barren, does not reveal either himself or others.

Yet there are plenty of great diaries left. There are the historical diaries, which suggest and convey the intimate spirit of whole periods and epochs far better, far more vividly than any formal historian can ever do. There is Greville. How the Georges and the Williams and the Wellingtons and the Peels and the Broughams live in his pages. There is our own John Quincy Adams, often indeed ponderously reflective and diffuse, but giving Jefferson and Clay and Burr and himself and a score of others a singular vitality. There is Saint-Simon, not strictly a diarist, but evidently writing his Memoirs from notes that glow with the heat of immediate observation. He may misrepresent, he may betray; but, oh, with what ardor does he give us the heart-beat of great kings and wayward ladies and scheming priests, and the color and splendor and glamour of a moving world!

And again, there are the literary diaries, which perform the same kindly — or unkindly — service for men of letters. There is the Goncourt Diary, with its intensely brilliant, if sometimes cruel and prejudiced portrayal of the writers who glorified France in the middle of the nineteenth century. Take the earlier group there depicted, Sainte-Beuve, Gautier, Renan, Taine. Lovers of Sainte-Beuve will find much to offend them in Goncourt's analysis of the great critics' scepticisms and cynicisms; but they will also find much that cries out from the canvas with the utmost vivacity of evident truth. *"Et son petit geste dessinait dans le vide des regrets de choses."* [10] All one side of Sainte-Beuve is in that touch. Take Zola and Daudet and Turgenev, all discussing in hushed oppression the haunting dread of death: [11] plenty of human nature there. And the Diary of Moore, lighter and more superficial, has yet glimpses of Scott and Byron and Wordsworth and Southey and a dozen others, which no one should miss.

But of all forms of diary the most interesting to persons who have the passion for human nature is undoubtedly the introspective, that in which the eye is constantly turned inwards in painful, anxious study of

16

the spiritual processes in the writer's soul. Without doubt such a preoccupation is abnormal. "I am always concerned with what is taking place within me," says Maine de Biran.[12] We are not made to live in that way. Perhaps it would be better for us to be no more conscious of our mental than of our physical interior. For instance, with Amiel, the most remarkable example of the type, the excess of contemplation and analysis blights action, blights the common external interest and usefulness of life. The whole universe is sicklied o'er with the pale cast of thought, melted, distilled, dissolved to a gray uniformity in which nothing stands out but one's self and God, and even God is apt to become shadowy beside the colossal predominance of the other element. Moreover, with all the immense analysis, it cannot be pretended that these cunning self-observers always get a veracious or satisfying result. With every intention of exactitude, they are too apt to distort, to exaggerate, to over-emphasize and to emphasize wrongly: they are always too near the object for perspective. One has constantly to check their observation by comparison with more healthy and normal subjects.

Yet, however such diarists may injure themselves and mislead their readers, their fascination remains, and if you understand the necessary corrections, their record is of enormous value. It is apt to be morbid and gloomy, partly because of a natural disposition in the writers, and partly in the sense of Emerson's excellent remark: "Why has my motley diary no jokes? Because it is a soliloquy, and every man is grave alone." [13] But the fascination far outweighs the gloom. Even in the more objective historical diarists I confess that what charms me most is the personal analysis, Greville's remorse over his waste of time and money in horse-racing, Adams's passionate desire to achieve as an author the distinction which has come to him so amply in the field of politics. Is not the following a charming bit of human nature to emanate from solemn John Quincy? "I was from dinner time until past two in the morning absorbed in the perusal of my own lectures, without a conception of the lapse of time, until at the close of the first volume, upon looking at my watch, I saw with astonishment the hour. What a portion of my life would I give if they could occasion the same accident to one other human being!" [14]

But, candid as these other diarists may be in confessing all the movement of their inner lives, the candor of no one of them approaches that of Pepys. Perhaps, on the whole, those who have most of his inimitable self-abandon are the two very different Americans, Samuel Sewall and Aaron Burr. But even the naïveté of Sewall's wooing of the Widow Winthrop and Burr's delightful baring of his miscellaneous amours pale beside the magnificent indiscretions of their English competitor. And of course the first inquiry one makes as to such a self-accusing and almost self-destroying record is, why did he do it?

Pepys himself helps us little to explain this puzzle. The use of a shorthand practically amounting to cipher indicates a desire for secrecy, which indeed was indispensable, since an indiscreet perusal of his record might have brought him to the gallows. The clear consciousness of some definite object would seem to be implied in the laborious performance of a daily task sufficiently extensive to produce eight solid printed volumes in a period of ten years and relinquished only because imperfect vision made it difficult and dangerous. Yet the Diarist never enlarges upon the point, indeed rarely refers to the Diary at all, which of itself illustrates his indisposition to indulge in deliberate theoretical self-analysis. The record, as we have it, begins abruptly, "Blessed be God, at the end of the last year I was in very good health, without any sense of my old pain, but upon taking of cold." [15] This seems to justify Mr. Wheatley's assumption of some sort of an earlier journal which might have proved more enlightening.[16] When there is imminent danger of an invasion, Pepys takes particular pains to rescue his papers, among others, "my journalls, which I value much." [17] But what he valued them for he does not say. Probably the chief conscious intention was the usefulness and later interest of record, at the back of which was the craving for self-expression which we have considered above. In view of the character of the Diary itself, most critics reject entirely any thought of publication. Nevertheless, I believe the vague shadow of it was there, and I find a hint of it in Pepys's remark, when Sir William Coventry confides his habit of keeping a journal of "the material things": "Upon which I told him, and he is the only man I ever told it to, I think, that I kept it most strictly these eight or ten years; and I am sorry almost that I told it him, it not being necessary, nor may be convenient, to have it known." [18] Whatever the motive, millions of readers have occasion to be grateful.

III

In the study of the Diary our first object is necessarily the soul of the writer. But it must not be forgotten that, quite independent of this interest, we are dealing with one of the most curious and valuable of historical documents, one from which historians have drawn and will draw, so long as they discuss the Restoration period. For Pepys had not only the passion for recording, he had the passion for seeing and hearing; and when the gifts of expression and of observation go together, the diarist is bound to give the world treasures of fact, or if it may sometimes be disputed as fact, at any rate treasures of suggestion.

Oh, that delight in observing the human heart, how inexhaustible it is in material, how inexhaustible in variety! And the masters of such observation, how tireless they are in research, how resourceful in finding or making opportunities. The chief of them all is perhaps Saint-Simon. With what intense relish does he enlarge upon the facility given him to plunge into the recesses of the soul and how eager he is to make use of it, "to pierce with my clandestine glances every feature, every gesture, every movement, and to satiate my curiosity with them." [19] When you read his ecstasies on the subject, you feel sometimes as if he were a hunter fiercely keen in following his prey, and it seems as if he gorged and glutted himself at the ample banquet of human nature. God knows that, after a certain age, it is the nourishment most acceptable to a debilitated digestion.

Pepys is perhaps less high-wrought in the expression of his ardor than Saint-Simon, but the ardor is none the less fundamental and sincere. He has affairs of his own that absorb him, but that does not prevent his having a wide-open eye and ear for all the strange accidents of life. "I, as I am in all things curious,"[20] he says, and as to one significant happening, "it is a most extraordinary thing to observe, and that which I would not but have had the observation of for a great deal of money."[21] Even when an occurrence is wearisome or tragic, there may be much matter to be learned from it. "The most horrible spectacles," says Saint-Simon, "have often instants of ridiculous contrast."[22] And Pepys remarks of a play of the Duchess of Newcastle's: "I was sick to see it, but yet would not but have seen it, that I might the better understand her."[23] While nothing excites the wonder and disgust of this inveterate sight-seer more than the bored indifference of a casual visitor to London: "But, Lord! what a stir Stankes makes with his being crowded in the streets and wearied in walking in London, and would not be wooed by my wife and Ashwell to go to a play, nor to White Hall, or to see the lyons, though he was carried in a coach. I never could have thought there had been upon earth a man so little curious in the world as he is."[24]

And seeing all this perplexed, entangled, highly colored hurly-burly of life, he turns to his Diary and sets it down, not with ordered rhetoric or systematic precision, but in a tumultuous hurly-burly which marvellously reflects the fascinating confusion of the spectacle itself. There are the great people of the world, how often they are little people, how often they are common people, how always they are human people, just like Samuel Pepys and you and me. There is a great king, whom Pepys saw and almost touched from day to day. And others may have been impressed with his greatness, with his stateliness, with the crown and robes and ermine. And these things impressed Pepys also, at suitable times. But there were other times of humble, frail humanity, which the observer appreciated with a certain satisfaction: "He told me several particulars of the King's coming thither, which was mighty pleasant, and shews how mean a thing a king is, how subject to fall, and how like other men he is in his afflictions." [25] And there is a poor queen, brought all the way from Portugal, a sovereign — and an outcast — among strangers in language, in religion, and in manners, who finds her husband flitting away from her to every new fair face that chooses to woo him. And Pepys gives the one word that sums up her life. When the waiting woman says, "I wonder your Majesty can have the patience to sit so long a-dressing," the queen answers: "I have so much reason to use patience, that I can very well bear with it." [26] It should be noted, by the way, that Pepys is not greatly given to quoting verbally, and it is one of the significant evidences of his veracity. Some diarists, Madame D'Arblay, for example, will set down long conversations, though we all know that to remember these exactly is quite impossible. Pepys does not betray us in any such fashion.

And right beside the kings and queens and great lords and fair ladies, the judges and generals and admirals and chancellors, each one distinguished and touched off with the fine vital mark that gives him his own individuality forever, there is the crowd of lesser people, plain men and women, who yet have for the observer their significance and curiosity, just because they are men and women. Take one of the officials of the Tower: "But, Lord! to see what a young, simple, fantastique coxcombe is made Deputy Governor, would make one mad; and how he called out for his night-gown of silk, only to make a show to us; and yet for half an hour I did not think he was the Deputy Governor, and so spoke not to him about the business, but waited for another man." [27] Or we have a brief, delightful, pathetic obituary: "This morning I hear that last night Sir Thomas Teddiman, poor man! did die by a thrush in his mouth: a good man, and stout and able, and much lamented." [28]

In this vague, vivid welter of dancing, shifting figures some — alas, too few — stand out as exceptionally good, and others as ridiculous or hateful. And it should be remarked that Pepys never strikes one as being naturally critical or censorious. He is ready to recognize goodness and charm wherever he finds them, and also remorseless in pointing out their opposites. It is life that is at fault, not he. So there is Mr. Hill, "my friend the merchant, that loves musique and comes to me a' Sundays, a most ingenious and sweet-natured and highly accomplished person." [29] And there is Evelyn, whom Pepys loved and praised, "a fine, a most excellent person he is." [30] Yet even here the remorseless eye and pen will work: "He read me part of a play or two of his making, very good, but not as he conceits them, I think, to be." [31] While, over against these estimable characters there are the foolish and the wicked, made just as lifelike and just as clinging as the others. There are the foolish, like the Backewell pair: "I do, contrary to my expectation, find her something a proud and vain-glorious woman, in telling the number of her servants and family and expences: he is also so, but he was ever of that strain;" [32] or, there is Povy: "he is

25

a coxcomb, and, I doubt, not over honest, by some things which I see; and yet, for all his folly, he hath the good lucke, now and then, to speak his follies in as good words, and with as good a show, as if it were reason, and to the purpose, which is really one of the wonders of my life." [33] And there are the wicked, like Lady Peters, who, when Pepys endeavors to mollify her as to an enemy, declares that "she would not, to redeem her from hell, do anything to release him; but would be revenged while she lived, if she lived the age of Methusalem." [34]

As a background to these vivid individual figures we must set the general picture of manners, which Pepys makes all the more real and telling, because he paints it, not of set purpose nor with elaborately studied effects, but by quick, bare, sudden touches and bits of intense observation and rendering. There is the political world, the old spirit of England laboring to adjust itself and sustain itself under new conditions. There is the hatred and rivalry of the Dutch, there is the jealousy of the French. There are the different quarrelsome elements in the country itself, the stern old Puritans, the fantastic cavaliers of the past, the pushing, eager politicians of the present. Those who govern are selfish, corrupt, worse still, perhaps, heedless, careless, unsystematic.

The people suffer, murmur, are ill-paid and unemployed, sometimes endure in silence, and sometimes pour out their discontent in sullen grumbling, so well portrayed in the wonderful page which Pepys writes under date of June 14, 1667, in the threat of invasion: "It is said they did in open streets yesterday, at Westminster, cry, 'A Parliament! A Parliament!' and I do believe it will cost blood to answer for these miscarriages." [35]

And all the time the court amuses itself. From the idle, witty, worthless king down to the meanest page in waiting pleasure, wantonness, waste, folly, and love-making are all that count. The watchful critic exposes these things with the finer understanding, perhaps also with the more regret, because he sympathizes with them himself. The men fight and make love. The women dress and make love. The Memoirs of Grammont depict it all with a sprightliness and literary grace which Pepys had not at his command. But we find in the Diary a terrible sincerity, a cool, unadorned, direct, fierce transcription of the vagaries of vice and folly, which no mere literary artifice could ever approach. There is the quiet, simple statement as to causes, which Matthew Arnold loved to quote, as a summing up of his great, aristocratic barbarian class: "At all which I am sorry; but it is the effect of idleness, and having nothing else to employ their great spirits upon." [36] There is the grim, gay, parti-colored sequence of effects. Now it is a brief picture of a thoughtless, vulgar frolic: "What mad freaks the Mayds of Honour at Court have: that Mrs. Jenings, one of the Duchesse's mayds, the other day dressed herself like an orange wench and went up and down and cried oranges; till falling down, or by such accident, though in the evening, her fine shoes were discerned, and she put to a great deale of shame." [37] Now it is an ugly summary of the courtiers' talk: "Their discourse, it seems, when they are alone, is so base and sordid, that it makes the eares of the very gentlemen of the back-stairs to tingle to hear it spoke in the King's hearing; and that must be very bad indeed." [38] Or perhaps a disappointed suitor says of the sacred precincts: "'If there be a hell, it is here. No faith, no truth, no love, nor any agreement between man and wife, nor friends.' He would have spoke broader, but I put it off to another time; and so parted." [39] And the little incident of the moth in a great crisis of England's history crowns the whole: "Sir H. Cholmly come to me this day, and tells me the Court is as mad as ever; and that the night the Dutch burned our ships the King did sup with my Lady Castlemayne, at the Duchess of

Monmouth's, and they were all mad in hunting a poor moth." [40]

So much for the court and high society. But Pepys's pages are even fuller of the daily life of the common world, which he met and studied on more even terms. There is the church, of which he is a constant and curious, if not very devout frequenter. The service and the sermon and the music and the frocks and the pretty girls are all recorded for us with equal fidelity. There is the theatre, the crowding press of that hungry mob, so long denied its natural entertainment, feeding its eyes and ears eagerly on the mock presentation of human passion and laughter. There are the London streets, thronged forever with anxious faces, merry faces, wanton faces, careless faces, wicked faces. Not a face escapes this man's attentive vision, and the most notable are handed on to us. And there is the home life, the manners and the morals and the passions and the money, gaiety, and generosity, pride and meanness, all stuff to weave into the thick, motley, human fabric of one's diary, if one is faithful enough, and perhaps foolish enough, to keep one.

There is the country life, which Pepys surveys somewhat afar off, in the spirit of the citizen's wife in "A King and No King": "Lord, how fine the fields be! What sweet living 'tis in the country!"[41] And again, "Poor souls, God help 'em, they live as contentedly as one of us." And Pepys's verdict on simple country sights is: "It brought those thoughts of the old age of the world in my mind for two or three days after."[42] There is the city life, with its bustle, and its noises, and its merriment; its lotteries, its cock-fights, its man-fights, which Pepys surveys with a mixture of delight and apprehension, such as we all remember in our youth: "It was pleasant to see, but that I stood in the pit, and feared that in the tumult I might get some hurt."[43] Oh, bewitching, enthralling, hideous, complicated world! And finally, over this daily run of monotonous, diverting humanity, brood the great, horrible London catastrophes, the fire and the plague. And Pepys's renderings of these, too long and elaborate to quote, at times hold the reader benumbed in the intensity of horror.

Pepys's simple, natural, sincere manner is evidently not calculated to sustain great, highly wrought scenes of dramatic effect, such as Saint-Simon delights in and carries off so wonderfully, the deaths of the royal princes, the degradation of the bastards, or, briefer, the celebrated incident of Louis XIV at the carp-pond.[44] Yet the English writer has his own triumphs in this kind, all the more telling for his vivid simplicity. Take the execution of the regicide Harrison: "Went out to Charing Cross, to see Major-general Harrison hanged, drawn, and quartered; which was done there, he looking as cheerful as any man could do in that condition. He was presently cut down, and his head and heart shown to the people, at which there was great shouts of joy. It is said, that he said that he was sure to come shortly at the right hand of Christ to judge them that now had judged him; and that his wife do expect his coming again." [45] Could there be a quieter, deeper touching of the human heart? Only his wife, out of the whole world, do expect his coming again.

IV

IT is touches like this that show the really great literary quality of the Diary of Pepys. Some critics, misled by the haste, the crudeness, the irregularity almost approaching illiteracy, have contested the literary value of the record altogether. What attracts us, they say, is simply the quaintness, the oddity, the almost childlike disregard of finish and correction. Well, there is a charm in the quaintness, no doubt. Pepys writes somewhat as we all think, brokenly, incoherently, with repetitions and lapses and omissions, an indifference to grammar, an in-

31

difference to formal logic. And this immediate transcription of thought gives an added, intense impression of fresh veracity, which startles us and keeps us awake and forever on the watch. The real lover of the Diary loves every imperfection and incompleteness in it, as so much evidence of its individuality and absolute truth. Even the set phrases, which recur day after day with what ought to be wearisome monotony, come to have their attraction. "So to bed, so to bed." It finishes the daily record, shuts and marks off a page of life. We are not content till we come to it, and feel that we can tuck up the wayward Diarist, like an invalid or a tired child.

But it is a serious error to suppose that Pepys was not a great stylist, because he was not a careful one. The same error might involve Shakespeare. Even the quaintness springs largely from lack of restraint, from throwing off convention, the tedious effort to write like other people, which has come to make so much writing of our own time gray and colorless. Pepys had an extraordinary gift for conveying just what he saw and felt, just as he saw and felt it.

It is not that he indulges in elaborate literary devices. He has few formal figures, he has few clever turns of rhetoric. The movement of his sentences is simple and direct, the stuff of them is vigorous, homely Saxon English, such as the humblest reader can understand. But the phrases hit you sensibly and hard. The homespun words give the color of the world, sometimes with a bald, glaring, simple intensity, sometimes with a glamorous richness. Take what one well-placed, daring word will do: "I find him one of the most *distinct* men that ever I did see in my life." [46] Take the power of conveying subjective experiences vividly, almost grossly: "Thus we end this month, as I said, after the greatest *glut of content* that ever I had." [47] Or again, the power of conveying them dreamily, with the utmost delicacy: "But I in such fear that I could not sleep till we came to Erith, and there it begun to be calm, and the stars to shine, and so I began to take heart again, and the rest too, and so made shift to slumber a little." [48]

Also, in the objective world, common, trivial matters stand out with a clear-cut definiteness that makes us appreciate the startling reality with which this instinctive seer saw them: "Lord! How I used to adore that man's talke, and now methinks he is but an ordinary man, his son a pretty boy indeed, but his nose unhappily awry." [49] Again, "rode to Impington, where I found my old uncle sitting all alone, like a man out of the world: he can hardly see; but all things else he do pretty livelyly." [50] And these

33

figures are set in a background of the inanimate, sketched with light, brief touches, yet sketched so that it clings in the memory: "It is strange what weather we have had all this winter; no cold at all; but the ways are dusty, and the flyes fly up and down, and the rose-bushes are full of leaves, such a time of the year as was never known in this world before here. This day many more of the Fifth Monarchy men were hanged." [51]

In order to show the effect produced on a larger scale by this irrelevant, immediate, direct, almost incoherent method of narrative, we must have one more extensive quotation. What formal, academic, ordered procedure could equal it? "By and by newes is brought to us that one of our horses is stole out of the stable, which proves to be my uncle's, at which I am inwardly glad — I mean, that it was not mine; and at this we were at a great loss; and they doubting a person that lay at next door, a Londoner, some lawyer's clerk, we caused him to be secured in his bed, and other care to be taken to seize the horse; and so about twelve at night or more, to bed in a sad, cold, nasty chamber, only the mayde was indifferent handsome, and so I had a kiss or two of her, and I to bed, and a little after I was asleep they waked me to tell me that the horse was found, which was good newes, and so to sleep till the morning, but was bit cruelly, and nobody else of our company, which I wonder at, by the gnats." [52]

But the height of Pepys's power of artistic rendering is reached in two passages, one of which will mean more to us later. The other, like the above, is a simple narrative of travel, rising to a point of poetical effect, which is all the more impressive because it is difficult to analyze: "And so away to Stevenage, and staid till a showre was over, and so rode easily to Welling, where we supped well, and had two beds in the room and so lay single, and still remember it that of all the nights that ever I slept in my life I never did pass a night with more epicurism of sleep; there being now and then a noise of people stirring that waked me, and it was a very rainy night, and then I was a little weary, that what between waking and then sleeping again, one after another, I never had so much content in all my life, and so my wife says it was with her." [53] Epicurism of sleep! Oh, magical phrase, to weary limbs and life-belabored souls! Epicurism of sleep!

And thus we see that this matchless unveiler of his own spirit had strange gifts and subtleties and resources of expression for accomplishing his object; but the expression matters little to us, compared with

35

the object; for do we not all spend life, instinctively or consciously, wandering up and down the wide world, endeavoring to touch even one other of these vague, elusive human souls, which seem to flit, forever mocking, just beyond our grasp? And few indeed are so tangible and approachable as the soul of Samuel Pepys.

II

PEPYS AND HIS OFFICE

I

DURING the Diary years, at any rate, Pepys's main occupation and engrossing interest was naturally his naval duties. These were altogether peaceful and, as we have seen, in the main confined to the land service. As a sailor, he was perhaps hardly more efficient than Sir Joseph Porter, and while he made occasional longer or shorter sea-excursions, his sea-legs could not be entirely relied on: "The ship (though the motion of it was hardly discernible to the eye) did make me sick, so as I could not eat anything almost." [1]

But on land and in the routine of the naval establishment he was a most important figure, and even so early as 1663 the King exclaimed, on meeting him, "Here is the Navy Office." [2] His functions were evidently of a varied character. Perhaps the most prominent of them were in connection with money. The general course of the accounting seems to have been subject to his vigilance, which was patient and unceasing: "Up early, my mind full of business, then to the office, where the two Sir Williams and I spent the morning passing the victualler's accounts." [3]

37

And if accounts were to be kept and money to be handled, it had to come from somewhere. Where it was to come from was an acute concern to Pepys, as it has been to many a public official similarly situated. The newly restored sovereign had demands upon him of all kinds, among which his own pleasures and amusements were not the least. Such money as he could wrest from Parliament was apt to be expended on these; and more essential, but remote, needs, like the Navy, were too frequently slighted. Pepys, with his conscientious vision and appreciation of a thousand indispensable requirements, sees the waste and deplores it; but there is little that he can do to help. What can be done by saving, he will attend to, so far as possible, and when contracts are made it is his first care that the government shall not be cheated: "There met several tradesmen by our appointment to know of them their lowest rates that they will take for their several provisions that they sell to us, for I do resolve to know that, and to buy no dearer, that so, when we know the lowest rate, it shall be the Treasurer's fault, and not ours, that we pay dearer." [4]

But, however the money is gained or saved, it has to be paid, paid, paid, payments for supplies, payments for wages, and when these latter are scanted there is trouble and discontent, and as often as not Pepys had to bear the blame, or at any rate get the grumbling. And the women were the worst, crying and complaining, till "I do most heartily pity them, and was ready to cry to hear them, but cannot helpe them. However when the rest were gone, I did call one to me that I heard complaine only and pity her husband and did give her some money, and she blessed me and went away." [5]

No doubt, besides this perpetual attempt to remedy the irremediable, there was much that was constructive also. There were stores and supplies to be investigated and provided, there were ships to be inspected, involving pleasant little outings to quaint seaports rife with adventure, there were always men to be dealt with, rough, bluff sea-captains, who swore great, dreadful oaths, and could not be brought to regard a landsman, even in authority, as of very much consequence, tarry sailors, who were even less dignified and less respectful, but whose salt and boisterous manners could not but tease such a timid official spirit with a strange, exotic enchantment.

And we have the remorseless daily record of the Clerk's attendance upon all these duties, his neglect, his failure, his disgust, but still his persistent attendance. To begin with, he lived in the building that

held his office, which is an unfortunate circumstance
for any one, so that he could rarely have associated
real homelike rest with that much-frequented abode
between Crutched Friars and Seething Lane. Such
an arrangement means business at all hours, at any
hour, with some sorts of temperaments at no hour.
And this was not Pepys's temperament, but home
matters sometimes distracted him. Then the work
itself involved being much abroad, and to a curious
eye there were a thousand diversions that tended to
interfere with labor. You meet a captain or a con-
tractor, and you take him to dinner or to the theatre,
and it is all most pleasant, and it may all tend to the
good of the Navy: who can say?

Also, there is the fundamental human disinclina-
tion to a set duty, whatever it be. "It is not that I
am idle in my nature neither," says the great and
vastly industrious Sir Walter. "But propose to me to
do one thing, and it is inconceivable the desire I have
to do something else." [6] Neither Sir Walter nor any
one has ever expressed this natural reluctance to duty
more vividly or generally than Samuel Pepys: "To
the office, where all the afternoon late, writing my
letters and doing business, but, Lord! what a conflict
I had with myself, my heart tempting me 1,000 times
to go abroad about some pleasure or other, notwith-

standing the weather foule. However, I reproached myself with my weaknesse in yielding so much my judgment to my sense, and prevailed with difficulty and did not budge, but stayed within, and, to my great content, did a great deale of business." [7]

But, in spite of temptations and distractions, there is no doubt of Pepys's punctuality and assiduity. He reprehends the performance of others: "in which so much laziness, as also in the Clerkes of the Cheque and Survey as that I do not perceive that there is one-third of their duties performed." [8] He frankly confesses the pretence of business when he is doing none, being unwilling to ride out in the coach with his wife, "afraid, at this busy time, to be seen with a woman in a coach, as if I were idle." [9] Yet his constant implication of faithfulness is even more impressive than the assertion of it, and fully bears out his noble account to Lady Carteret of his persistence during the plague: "I have stayed in the city . . . till my very physician, Dr. Burnet, who undertook to secure me against any infection, having survived the month of his own house being shut up, died himself of the plague; till the nights, though much lengthened, are grown too short to conceal the burials of those that died the day before, people being thereby constrained to borrow daylight for the service; lastly,

through your hands at one time or another, and to understand them takes a vast amount of effort for a man who would like to get an occasional hour for amusing himself. Nay, we have even to have a knowledge of topography, to be familiar with the lay of the land and the lay of the water: otherwise we may be fooled and the service may suffer: "I do perceive that I am very short in my business by not knowing many times the geographical part of my business." [13]

Unquestionably there is interest in it all: "My head has not been so full of business a great while, and with so much pleasure, for I begin to see the pleasure it gives." [14] But there is fatigue, also, wearing journeys and exhausting vigils, and constant friction with intractable and tedious persons. And there is endless and unescapable worry and anxiety. There is worry about public affairs, the extreme need of efficient service and the impossibility of getting it. There is worry about one's own position, the difficulty of filling it satisfactorily, and the difficulty of retaining it, when one is too dependent upon the favor and influence of those whose own tenure is fragile beyond belief. If one happens to be of a worrying temperament, these things bite like gnats and it is hard to brush them away. And Samuel Pepys was of a worrying temperament, and knew it: "I all that night so vexed that I did not sleep almost all night, which shows how unfit I am for trouble." [15] And again, "Not that I fear him at all, but the natural aptness I have to be troubled at any thing that crosses me." [16]

It will at once be asked, what health had the man to bear all these strains and burdens and vexations. It would appear that he was constitutionally vigorous enough, and indeed he must have been, to live as he lived to the good age of seventy. One pictures him as a robust, sturdy, stocky, English figure, firmly planted on a pair of legs meant for service as well as dignity. He congratulates himself upon his general freedom from fatigue: "So to bed very weary, which I seldom am." [17] And in age he insists that he has been careless of his physical condition: "I have always been too little regardful of my own health, to be a prescriber to others." [18]

But when a man has had a severe illness in his youth, it is apt to leave him more or less self-conscious in such matters. Even when he tries to be reckless, he cannot be so altogether. When Pepys was twenty-five years old, he was cut for the stone, and the operation, as was natural, left a serious impress on his life. With thoroughly characteristic curiosity, he kept the stone which had been removed, even treasured it with a sort of reverence. Six years afterward he goes with a friend "to look out a man to make a case, for to keep my stone, that I was cut of, in." [19] Also, he honored the anniversary of the event, when he could, gathered his friends to make a feast of celebration, and was anxious to remember the past with gratitude and to avoid a relapse in the future.

As a result of this experience, the Diary contains a luxuriant record of symptoms and precautions and remedies, which might be tedious, if it were not so splendidly human. Pepys takes chances on eating and drinking, to which he was confessedly rather inclined, as you would take them, and congratulates himself if he comes out alive, as you would. And perhaps he takes them again, and is much less lucky, and bewails his folly, and makes good resolutions. And then the temptations come and the old story is repeated. And we know it so well. Yet it is always new.

But in sickness or health there is the office waiting. And we have seen that Pepys had fidelity and industry. Yet neither of these finally avails without the instinct of order and system. I think we are justified in concluding that the Diarist had this instinct in a marked degree. The thoroughness and care which he evinces in the management of his own affairs and the

46

constant and zealous watchfulness with which he examines and arranges such public matters as come within his province are a sufficient proof of it. Assuredly he had enough occasion to criticize and blame the lack of system in others, and in his intimate record he is not sparing of such criticism. He inspects the stores and finds them abundant, but not handled or superintended with any care. "Then to Woolwich, and viewed well all the storehouses, and then to Mr. Ackworth's and Sheldon's to view their books, which we found not to answer the King's service and security at all as to the stores." [20] He bewails the want of discipline: a fellow-official "complains and sees perfectly what I with grief do, and said it first himself to me, that all discipline is lost in the fleete, no order nor no command." [21] Shiftlessness, irregularity, and irresponsibility in the office anger him to the heart: "This added to my former disquiet, made me stark mad, considering all the nakedness of the office lay open in papers within those covers. I could not tell in the world what to do, but was mad on all sides, and that which made me worse Captain Cocke was there, and he did so swear and curse at the boy that told me." [22]

Also, it is pretty to see how in two points most indispensable to system, self-control, and the firm

47

power of saying no, this inveterate self-critic commends and arraigns himself. For in regard to a pleasant piece of news he says: "I did never more plainly see my command of my temper in my not admitting myself to receive any kind of joy from it till I had heard the certainty of it." [23] And, on the other hand, he bewails his own weakness: "I (who in my nature am mighty unready to answer no to anything, and thereby wonder that I have suffered no more in my life by my easiness in that kind than I have) answered him that I would do it." [24]

II

HERE is where the element of human contact comes in, and this side of Pepys's official life is by no means the least interesting. For he was daily thrown with all sorts of people, high and low, good and bad, rough and gentle, and his success in the world, as with so many of us, depended more upon his skill and tact in these relations than upon anything else whatever.

With his superiors his attitude, so far as we can judge from the Diary, seems to be in the main creditable, allowing for the importance of rank in those days and the immense distance that was established and recognized between a mere common man and the great ones of the earth. He did his work, and did it well, and knew that he did, and while he realized that the hold upon a public position depended upon other things as well as worth, he did not propose to cringe or flatter unduly. With his immediate chief in the Navy Department, the Duke of York, his relation seems always to have been most satisfactory. James spoke to him and of him with respect and consideration. Pepys records one of these compliments with much content: "He did tell me how much I was beholding to the Duke of York, who did yesterday of his own accord tell him that he did thank him for one person brought into the Navy, naming myself, and much more to my commendation, which is the greatest comfort and encouragement that ever I had in my life." [25] No doubt this agreeable state of things was fostered by a good deal of self-restraint. "So that I am well at present with him, but I must have a care not to be over-busy in the office again, and burn my fingers," remarks the watchful subordinate in regard to another somewhat sensitive superior.[26] And he is careful to cultivate a large discretion as to appearances. When asked by the Duke on one occasion where he was going in a barge, "I told him to Woolwich, but was troubled afterward I should say no farther, being in a gally, lest he think me too profuse in my journeys." [27]

But it must not for a moment be supposed that the glamour of crowns or purple drapery dazzles or obfuscates the keen vision of this acute observer and critic. And here I am again reminded of that poor Fanny Burney, who was certainly no fool, but for whom majesty was sacred and the great shadow of a diadem obscured all faults. George the Third might be a mad egotist to the rest of the world; he was a crowned idol to her. How far, far different is the case with Pepys. He tumbles off the crown, and strips off the robe, and under the royal insignia sees just plain, bare human flesh, no better than most, far worse than much. And then he sums it all up with one of his unforgetable touches: "And so they parted, the King bidding him do as he would; which, methought, was an answer not like a King that did intend ever to do well." [28] Even dukes, though they so mightily commend us, have just that same frail flesh and blood at bottom, and if we are pushed, we must admit — well, what do you think we admit? "He told me that he did not think it was necessary for the Duke of York to do so, and that it would not suit so well with his nature nor greatness; which last, perhaps, is true, but then do too truly shew the effects of having Princes in places, where order and discipline should be." [29] As for the noisy and boisterous Rupert, a very few words suffice to dispose of him: "Prince Rupert do nothing but swear and laugh a little, with an oathe or two, and that's all he do." [30]

The supreme lesson that one learns in dealing with these great fellows is patience, to keep quiet and hold one's tongue and wait. "Among others to my Lord Treasurer's, there to speak with him, and waited in the lobby three long hours for to speake with him, to the trial of my utmost patience, but missed him at last, and forced to go home without it, which may teach me how I make others wait." [31] This is the sort of moral reflection we all indulge in and sometimes we profit by it and sometimes we do not. Did Pepys, in dealing with those subordinate to him?

Evidently his work was not in the main of an executive order. Mr. Morehouse commends his energy in suppressing drunkenness in the Navy. [32] But it does not appear that he had the direction or management of large bodies of men. I question whether he would have wholly succeeded in this. He was too self-critical and self-distrustful. Yet his clerks and assistants seem to have been efficient and devoted, at least if we may judge by the record and testimony of William Hewer, who remained not only an official associate, but a lifelong friend and was appointed his chief's sole executor with a bequest of five hundred pounds, "as a very small instance of my respect and most sensible esteem of his more than filial affection and tenderness expressed towards me through all the occurrences of my life for forty years past unto this day." [33]

When it came to a question of getting work done, Pepys believed in discipline and seeing that the proper person did it. A petty officer comes to him with a complaint: "I was angry; he told me I ought to give people ease at night, and all business was to be done by day. I answered sharply, that I did not make, nor any honest man, any difference between night and day in the King's business, and this was such." [34] And I am afraid that at times, like most of us, he let his temper get the better of him, when he felt that he could afford to do so: "Vexed to find Griffin leave the office door open, and had a design to have carried away the screw of the carpet in revenge to him, but at last I would not, but sent for him and chid him, and so to supper and to bed, having drank a great deal of wine." [35] But in the main I think he was inclined to be fair and friendly and considerate: "Though I did get another signed of my own clerk's, yet I will give it to his clerk, because I would not be judged un-kind." [36] Always, you see, the incomparable candor: "because I would not be *judged* unkind." How it appears in passage after passage: "It is my content that by several hands today I hear that I have the name of good-natured man among the poor people that come to the office." [37]

Indeed, it is a delight to see how quickly this sensitive temper responds to good and ill opinion. Or rather, he responds no more than we all do, but he admits it and records it, as we all do not. Slights, scorns, snubs, abuse, fret and depress him. "After dinner to Pay again, and so till 9 at night, my great trouble being that I was forced to begin an ill practice of bringing down the wages of servants, for which people did curse me, which I do not love." [38] Also, we must be careful to maintain our social status, or these lower sort of persons may have a contempt for us: "Here I was troubled to be seen by four of our office clerks, which sat in the half-crown box and I in the 1s, 6d." [39] On the other hand, how he does bask and expand in the respect and honor paid him as a distinguished public servant and a high official in His Majesty's Navy. There is the quiet deference that comes in the routine of daily business: "There find poor Mr. Spong walking at my door, where he had knocked, and being told I was at the office staid modestly there walking because of disturbing me, which methinks was one of the most modest acts (of a man that hath no need of being so to me,) that ever I knew in my life." [40] There is the obsequiousness of the vulgar, which in its novelty so overcomes us that we hardly know which way to look; but we grow bravely accustomed to it: "I find that I begin to know now how to receive so much reverence, which at the beginning I could not tell how to do." [41] Yes, even those terrible, swaggering captains, however the tongue may be in the cheek, are forced to pay mouth honor, bowing low their bluff marine supremacy: "Never till now did I see the great authority of my place, all the captains of the fleet coming cap in hand to us." [42] And when we go out into the great world, it is the same, and we observe it with some astonishment and exceeding joy: "Here a very brave dinner, though no invitation; and, Lord! to see how I am treated, that come from so mean a beginning, is matter of wonder to me." [43]

With his approximate equals and colleagues in his regular office work Pepys's experience was probably pretty much that of any public official, whose associates are thrust upon him rather than subject to his own choice and natural affinity. There were trials and rubs and friction, dark days and discouragements, times when it seemed impossible to get on and not worth while to try. You may even feel that this atmosphere of unpleasantness predominates and that the Diarist's mood towards his fellows is one of rather constant irritation. Yet there were agreeable moments and agreeable people, and the record is by no means barren or unappreciative of them. To be sure, it has been observed that only one of the numerous fellow-workers with whom Pepys was in daily contact is uniformly spoken well of, Sir William Coventry. One passage will give the usual tone in regard to him: "I find him the most ingenuous person I ever found in my life, and am happy in his acquaintance and my interest in him." [44] But, after all, if you set down with Pepys's utter honesty your opinion of the men you meet every day, would there be many of them with whom there were no reserves?

On the whole, it seems that he is fairly well satisfied with his personal relations. Even, in a sunshiny hour, he can survey them with a good deal of serenity: "Wherein I am a happy man, that all my fellow-officers are desirous of my friendship." [45] And this satisfactory status was undoubtedly maintained by a certain constitutional amiability, which might go the length of practical benefit, when it did not involve too much sacrifice: "I did walk a few turns with Commissioner Pett, and did give the poor weak man some advice for his advantage how to better his pleading for himself, which I think he will if he can remember and practise, for I would not have the man suffer what he do not deserve, there being enough of what he do deserve to lie upon him." [46]

Moreover, it is evident that the Clerk of the Acts had the faculty of working with others, even when he did not agree with them or approve of them. He knew something at least of the great practical secret of compromise, knew that the world's work is best forwarded by being ready to yield your own opinions, or to postpone the utterance of them to a favorable opportunity, that progress is obtained by being able to harmonize diverging and almost conflicting forces in a resultant that may be rough and irregular, but is at any rate in the right direction. If a man can tell you something useful about timber or about ships, you listen to him, even if you have not a high regard for his general wisdom or his official honesty. If a man is valuable for the public service or for your personal advancement, you cultivate his society, and reserve your private estimate of his character for those terrible hidden cipher pages: "It is my design to keep much in with Sir George; and I think I have begun very well towards it." [47] The assumption of a certain modesty, which perhaps you do not altogether feel, is likely to bring soothing compliments, and possibly more solid advantages: very well, let us assume it. "And when I

SAMUEL PEPYS

From the portrait by John Hayls in the National Portrait Gallery

said I was jealous of myself, that having now come to such an income as I am, by his favour, I should not be found to do as much service as might deserve it; he did assure me, he thinks it not too much for me, but thinks I deserve it as much as any man in England. All this discourse did cheer my heart, and sets me right again, after a good deal of melancholy." [48] If a colleague can cheer your heart by a little kindly praise, of a dark hour, his society is worth something.

Also, there is comfort in having some one with whom you can talk things over. Kings are wasteful, officials are shiftless, contractors are sordid, the world does at times seem to be going to the dogs. You get a friend in a quiet corner over a quart of wine and a barrel of oysters and the exchange of pessimisms does much to alleviate them, even if the good wine teases the tongue a little beyond discretion: "In the close he and I did fall to talk very openly of the business of this office, and (if I was not a little too open to tell him my interest, which is my fault) he did give me most admirable advice." [49]

But unquestionably the pulling and hauling of fragile human tempers among each other is wearing and exhausting, and, do the best you can, there are some men you hate the sight of, unreasonably, and some who bore you, just plain bore you, till you find them worse than the others. If you are a remorseless diarist, in the habit of confiding to your secret record things which must not, simply must not, be allowed to escape the bulwark of your teeth, some extraordinary reflections do get away from your unhampered pen. "I find that he is dead, and died this morning, at which I was much surprized; and indeed the nation hath a great loss; though I cannot, without dissembling, say that I am sorry for it, for he was man never kind to me at all." [50] Or again, "I am at a loss whether it will be better for me to have him die, because he is a bad man, or live, for fear a worse should come." [51]

There is the meanness of the world, men who will work day and night to get you out of a good place, or balk you of a good bargain. There is the wickedness of the world, men who will sacrifice the public service and their country, to save their own skins, or even a little inconvenience. There is the folly of the world, creatures like Sir John Minnes and Mr. Povy, set to manage great affairs, and blundering till one wonders why God ever created them: "In little, light, sorry things very cunning; yet, in the principal, the most ignorant man I ever met with in so great trust as he is." [52]

And sometimes one has to make one's way by sheer

adroitness, to keep out of quarrels and let others do
the fighting. And it cannot be denied that Pepys was
a master in this genial art. But there are occasions
when even he rebels. There comes a captain — one
of those imposing captains — who abuses an absent
subordinate most unjustly. Pepys resists, in good set
terms, "though all and the worst that I ever said was
that that was insolently or ill mannerdly spoken.
When he told me that it was well it was here that I
said it." [53] And a duel almost resulted. And Pepys
was worried over it: "This day though I was merry
enough, yet I could not get yesterday's quarrel out
of my mind, and a natural fear of being challenged
by Holmes for the words I did give him." [54] But it
was all averted by that generous peace-maker, an if.

Two figures are especially conspicuous in the friction and troubles that beset Pepys's official life, Sir
William Batten and Sir William Penn, the "Sir Williams both," who are mentioned in so many pages of
the Diary. Batten, though often intrusive and vexatious, does not appear to have caused very serious annoyance. But Penn, the father of the more celebrated
American William, was a bugbear at every turn.
Viewed in the testimony of others, he seems to have
been not only a highly competent seaman, but a useful Commissioner of the Navy, and if his public and

private morals were not always what they should be, whose were at that time? But Pepys was frankly jealous of him, of his social precedence, of his marine experience as a sea-going admiral, of his wealth, his standing, his comfortable establishment; and the jealousy appears in endless bursts of perhaps temporary irritation in the Diary. There is the wonderful page in which "Mrs. Turner and I sat up till 12 at night talking alone in my chamber, and most of our discourse was of our neighbors." [55] And the whole history and character of the Penn family are turned inside out and upside down, till there is hardly a decorous rag left to cover it. There is the quarrel scene, most intense and impressive of many: "Up, and to the Office, where sat all the morning and there a most furious conflict between Sir W. Pen and I, in a few words, and on a sudden occasion, of no great moment, but very bitter, and stared on one another, and so broke off, and to our business, my heart as full of spite as it could hold, for which God forgive me and him!" [56] Yet see the fundamental fairness of the man. After all the criticism and abuse, when Penn has a chance of advancement, Pepys cannot but approve: "I perceive he do look after J. Minnes's place if he dies, and though I love him not nor do desire to have him in, yet I do think he is the first man in England for it." [57]

III

As we have considered Pepys's practical qualifications
for his office-work and his more or less complicated relations with his fellows, so we must look at the moral
characteristics which appeared in the course of his
daily employment. The question of his honesty is a
difficult one, or rather it has to be viewed less in itself
than in connection with the standards and habits that
prevailed about him. Perhaps this is as true of a good
many men of business to-day as it was then.

In the abstract Pepys liked to speak the truth, and
meant to, and no doubt in the main did. The truth!
How many shades and turns and twists it has, and
how easy — as well as difficult — it is to reconcile
veracity with courtesy and comfort and profit. In his
own affairs he sometimes displays a nicety of conscience which charms as much as it surprises. For instance, there is the eternal torment of tax returns, as
vexatious three centuries ago as to-day. "Though
this be a great deal, yet it is a shame I should pay no
more; that is, that I should not be assessed for my
pay, as in the Victualling business and Tangier, and
for my money, which, of my own accord, I had determined to charge myself with £1,000 money, till coming to the Vestry, and seeing nobody of our ablest

merchants, as Sir Andrew Rickard, to do it, I thought it not decent for me to do it, nor would it be thought wisdom to do it unnecessarily, but vain glory." [58] Alas, how much the example of "our ablest merchants" is responsible for!

When it comes to criticizing the sins of his contemporaries, to setting forth the vices of the age with naked vividness, Pepys is as uncompromising as to money as in regard to other matters. Favoritism? Everybody shows favoritism. Profits? Everybody is on the lookout for profits. Bribes? Well, Mr. Cooling may incline to exaggerate, but his statement seems fairly typical: he "told us his horse was a bribe, and his boots a bribe; and told us he was made up of bribes, as an Oxford scholar is set out with other mens' goods when he goes out of town, and that he makes every sort of tradesman to bribe him; and invited me home to his house to taste of his bribe wine." [59]

In view of this general condition, we must agree heartily with Mr. Wheatley in regarding Pepys as essentially honest and even scrupulous. [60] He had plenty of enemies, as was natural, who made attacks upon his official honesty, as upon other things. An anonymous pamphlet, without date, called "An Outcry after P. and W. H.(ewer) and Plain Truth," [61] seems to be among the most virulent of these. But good authorities reject the more scandalous charges as absurd.[62] Many a doubtful bargain, many a suspicious percentage, came in Pepys's way. Some he rejected as questionable, or not even questionable, in themselves. Some he put aside with a sigh, as coming from sources which it was dangerous to deal with at all. The bribes popped up from all quarters, and it was so easy to slip a few pounds in your pocket and almost forget how they came there. The worst and most difficult cases to settle were those in which a considerable gain to yourself might very well accompany a substantial advantage to the public service. And in debating these there were endless chances for the most subtle and delightful casuistry. "This puts me upon thinking to offer something presently myself to prevent its being done in a worse manner without me relating to the Victualling business, which, as I may order it, I think may be done and save myself something." [63] But we must steel ourselves, we must be firm, above all, even at a small sacrifice, we must blight the wicked transactions of our associates: "Had a difference with Sir W. Batten about Mr. Bowyer's tarr, which I am resolved to cross, though he sent me last night, as a bribe, a barrel of sturgeon, which, it may be, I shall send back, for I will not have

63

the King abused so abominably in the price of what we buy, by Sir W. Batten's corruption and underhand dealing." [64]

Taking everything together, we feel justified in describing ourselves as one "who am known to be so far from needing any purgation in the point of selling places, as never to have taken so much as my fee for a commission or warrant to any one office in the Navy, within the whole time, now 20 years, that I have had the honor of serving his Majesty therein." [65]

And, though unquestionably Pepys had a wholesome human instinct of money-getting, there were other motives back of his industry and fidelity, besides mere financial acquisitiveness. He was normally ambitious, liked to get ahead in the world, to earn the respect of his fellows and receive it, to do good honest work and have the reward of it. He liked to look back at his humble beginnings and to realize the immense progress he had made, partly by his own earnest, persistent effort, partly by the blessing of Providence. "That I, from a mean clerke there, should come to strike tallys myself for that sum, and in the authority that I do now, is a very stupendous mercy to me." [66]

He was ambitious for distinction in general, liked the idea of Parliament when it came in his way, co-

quetted with it in the pretty fashion which is common
to us all, and declared that the satisfaction of having
discharged his duty was what he aimed at,[67] but
liked it, and was pleased when his friends approved of
his seeking such an honour.[68] Especially he was eager
for advancement in his office, looked onward and upward, made huge, strange, tiring efforts to achieve it,
tickled the great and tormented the little, spent long
days and anxious nights, hoped and despaired and
found out by bitter experience the harsh and thorny
nature of the mounting habits of the world.

And sometimes the discouragement and the difficulty seemed too great, the risks too appalling, so that
only a fool would let himself be involved in them.
Was there not country air to be had, and country
sounds and sights, and peace? "Played with pleasure, but with a heavy heart, only it pleased me to
think how it may please God I may live to spend
my time in the country with plainness and pleasure,
though but with little glory."[69] There are times
when the thought pleases all of us, or we imagine it
does. And then the city drags us back, the city and
the whirl of it, and the real business of men, and pride
and hope and ambition and pleasure, or the shadows
of all these things, which we follow till we die.

But it would be unfair to attribute Pepys's effort en-

65

tirely to the desire of profit and of personal distinction. There was a large, indisputable element of real patriotism and passion for public service and accomplishment. And it is pretty to see the man's shrewd analysis struggling to disentangle these complicated motives: "I laboured hard at Deering's business of his deals more than I would if I did not think to get something, though I do really believe that I did what is to the King's advantage in it, and yet, God knows, the expectation of profit will have its force and make a man the more earnest." [70] But the patriotism was there, all the same, and was genuine. It shows in his passionate sorrow over the decay and corruption that he saw around him and could do so little to remedy, "which is one of the saddest things that, at such a time as this, with the greatest action on foot that ever was in England, nothing should be minded, but let things go on of themselves, do as well as they can." [71] It shows in such sayings as his hearty agreement with Mr. Coventry's resolution, "never to baulke taking notice of any thing that is to the King's prejudice, let it fall where it will, which is a most grave resolucion." [72] It shows most of all in the determination to do his little bit, whenever and wherever he can, to forward the interests of his country, to make the Navy efficient, successful, and triumphant, and to that end to thwart intrigue and dishonesty and corruption, so far as it lies in his power. "There with my wife and W. Hewer, talking all the evening, my mind running on the business of the Office, to see what more I can do to the rendering myself acceptable and useful to all and to the King." [73]

And when one has done one's best, even if it be but little, and knows that one has, one likes to be commended and to have one's work appreciated. And what is the use of keeping an intimate diary, if one is not to record the compliments one gets? One enjoys the approval of the public, and frankly, without false modesty, one thinks one has deserved it: "Pierce tells me that all the town do cry out of our office, for a pack of fools and knaves; but says that everybody speaks either well, or at least the best of me, which is my great comfort, and think I do deserve it, and shall shew I have." [74] One enjoys the good word of one's colleagues. Mr. Coventry speaks well of me, and he ought to; but still it is pleasant. One enjoys, above all, the praise of one's superiors. When the Duke of York is lavish in laudation, it "do make me joyful beyond myself that I cannot express it, to see that as I do take pains, so God blesses me, and hath sent me masters that do observe that I take pains." [75]

But there was a day in Pepys's career beside which

all other days were insignificant, the fifth of March, 1668. The discontent of Parliament with the Navy had come to a head in the threat to turn out the principal officers and have a new order of things. The defence of his department fell upon Pepys and his speech was sufficient to avert the disaster. Yet what a day of anxiety it was and what a night of tumultuous thought beforehand. "Slept about three hours, but then waked, and never in so much trouble in all my life of mind, thinking of the task I have upon me, and upon what dissatisfactory grounds, and what the issue of it may be to me." [76]

And it is not known that Pepys was a great orator, or that in his later parliamentary period he achieved any special rhetorical distinction. But this time his heart was in it, and he triumphed. Compliments were showered upon him from every possible source, and no one could resist the charm of the naïve grace with which he sets them down. The whole account should be read and savoured, every bit of it. But the final sentence is surely a masterpiece of human ecstasy: "Mr. Ashburnham, and every creature I met there of the Parliament, or that knew anything of the Parliament's actings, did salute me with this honour:— Mr. Godolphin;— Mr. Sands, who swore he would go twenty mile, at any time, to hear the like again,

and that he never saw so many sit four hours together to hear any man in his life, as there did to hear
me; Mr. Chichly, — Sir John Duncomb," [note the
gasp of delight with which every fresh name is remembered, the words fall over each other in dis-
ordered revelry] "and everybody do say that the
kingdom will ring of my abilities, and that I have
done myself right for my whole life: and so Captain
Cocke, and others of my friends, say that no man
had ever such an opportunity of making his abilities
known; and, that I may cite all at once, Mr. Lieutenant of the Tower did tell me that Mr. Vaughan did
protest to him, and that, in his hearing it, said so to
the Duke of Albemarle, and afterwards to W. Coventry, that he had sat twenty-six years in Parliament and never heard such a speech there before: for
which the Lord God make me thankful! And that
I may make use of it not to pride and vain-glory,
but that, now I have this esteem I may do nothing
that may lessen it! I spent the morning thus walking in the Hall, being complimented by everybody
with admiration." [77] But somehow the tribute of
"Mr. Lieutenant of the Tower" especially touches
my heart.

Such days do not come often in any man's life, and
one thinks of the remark of Burke to Fanny Burney,

when he and Dr. Johnson had vied with each other for a whole evening in praising her, "Miss Burney, die to-night."

Note — A very cursory examination of the "Descriptive Catalogue of the Naval Manuscripts in the Pepysian Library," now in course of publication and edited by Mr. J. R. Tanner, will suffice to show the variety, the importance, and the high patriotic quality of the services rendered by Samuel Pepys to the English Navy. Mr. Tanner says, "Of the three thousand volumes of which the Pepysian Library consists, some two hundred and fifty are manuscripts, and of these about half are manuscript volumes relating to the navy." In his general introduction Mr. Tanner gives an extensive and detailed analysis of the significance of these documents and concludes: "From the Diary we learn that Pepys was a musician, a dandy, a collector of books and prints, a man of science, an observer of boundless curiosity, and, as one of his critics has pointed out, one who possessed an 'amazing zest for life.' From the Pepysian manuscripts we learn that he was a man of sound judgment, of orderly business habits and methods, of great administrative capacity and energy; and that he possessed extraordinary shrewdness and tact in dealing with men. It is the combination of these qualities that is little short of astounding, and if the bearing of the Pepysian papers on the personal character of Pepys is once realized, it will be impossible to belittle him any more." To which it should perhaps only be added that the practical business qualities may also be discerned in the Diary by the thoughtful and observant reader, and that such a reader will never have the disposition to belittle the Diarist.

III
PEPYS AND HIS MONEY
I

I HAVE said that Pepys had a wholesome human instinct for money-getting. No one who turns over the Diary can question this. Money formed a large part of the Diarist's life. Does it not form a large part of all our lives, however decorously we conceal it and endeavor to overlook it? "Getting and spending we lay waste our powers," says the poet. We use them in that way, at any rate. Pepys got and saved and spent and gave, like the rest of us, meanly say some, wisely say others, probably meanly and wisely both, like the rest of us. And, so doing, he managed to live in comfort, if not affluence, though he accumulated no very great fortune. Let us see how he did it.

To begin with, he appreciated the necessity of paying your debts, of not being in debt to any one for anything, when you could possibly help it. "I would have paid Mr. Hunt for it, but he did not come along with it himself, which I expected and was angry for it, so much is it against my nature to owe anything to any body." [1] Then he understood that the first secret of being well off in the world is to know precisely where you stand, to keep exact and systematic accounts. It may not be strictly true, as a great economist has said, that no bankrupt ever kept proper books and that no one who kept proper books was ever bankrupt. But it comes near to being a general rule, and Pepys knew it as well as anybody. Whether in private or public matters, he believes that the keeping of accounts means protection and salvation. "When I consider that a regular accountant never ought to fear any thing nor have reason, I then do cease to wonder." [2]

There is persistency. No matter how weary one is, no matter what may be the pressure of business or pleasure, those accounts must be kept in order. If one misses a day, one suffers for it and regrets it afterwards: "for I find that two days' neglect of business do give more discontent in mind than ten times the pleasure thereof can repair again, be it what it will." [3] There is regularity. No use in having a grand bout of adjustment once in two or three weeks or months. When the proper time comes, the work must be done and not put off till a more convenient season. If private affairs get crowded out by the duties of the office, private affairs must encroach upon sleep and even upon the Sabbath, may God forgive the profanation. There is detail. The pounds are made up of shillings and pennies, and the pennies may not be neglected, if the grand total is to be correct. And, however complicated and wearisome the calculation may be, it has got to be done: "Very late alone upon my accounts, but have not brought them to order yet, and very intricate I find it, notwithstanding my care all the year to keep things in as good method as any man can do." [4] Finally, you must do things yourself, not trust figures and records and returns to others, if you would avoid trouble: "This night I did even my accounts of the house, which I have to my great shame omitted now above two months or more, and therefore am content to take my wife's and mayd's accounts as they give them, being not able to correct them, which vexes me; but the fault being my own, contrary to my wife's frequent desires, I cannot find fault." [5]

And it makes a troubled and anxious life, no doubt. And there are persons who say that it is not worth while, that it is better to let the money come and go as it will and enjoy yourself. With all your care and all your worry, things may go wrong by unavoidable accident, and you will have had your misery for nothing. The Lord will provide for you, or your friends will, or somebody will, and meantime the sun shines, and life can be a very merry thing, if you let it. But persons of Pepys's temper are well aware that the sun does not shine always and life is not always so merry, and on the bad days a few dollars in the bank are immensely comforting. If you are born to worry, you will worry anyway, and why not about something useful?

But the worry is persistent and haunting and it is hard to shake it off. There is worry about immediate expenditure. Pepys feels that he ought to see his store pile up, increase regularly day by day and year by year. But somehow the shillings slip away and this thing and that thing entices, till it gets so that he is really afraid to figure up how he stands at all. And there is future possible expenditure. He must save, he must get ahead, he must prepare. His father is old and dependent, and his brothers and sisters must be provided for, and where is the money to come from? And then he will be old himself sometime, and he would like to feel that he will not have to be dependent upon any one. Yet how to accomplish it and at the same time have what he absolutely needs to-day? And he expresses such torment, in its mixture with little daily annoyances, with that extraordinary, inimitable faculty of touching off grief and trial as well as joy: "We missed also the surrenders of his copyhold land, without which the land would not come to us, but to the heir at law, so that what with this, and the badness of the drink and the ill opinion I have of the meat, and the biting of the gnats by night, and my disappointment in getting home this week, and the trouble of sorting all the papers, I am almost out of my wits with trouble, only I appear the more contented, because I would not have my father troubled." [6] And in general, the man is forced to admit, as we have seen, that he is inclined to worry and does not bear troubles as well as he might. Perhaps, after all, it will be found that the human family at large is not so very different from him. "This business of this fellow, though it may be a foolish thing, yet it troubles me, and I do plainly see my weakness that I am not a man able to go through trouble, as other men, but that I should be a miserable man if I should meet with adversity, which God keep me from!" [7]

We wish to know first whence Pepys derived his money. At the beginning of the Diary we find him with a small accumulation, drawn from careful saving. As he frankly puts it, "My own private condition very handsome, and esteemed rich, but indeed very poor." [8] When he sums up his affairs more precisely, he finds that he is worth forty pounds and more, which is better than he expected, and he fears that he has forgotten something. [9] A short time afterward, the total has risen to eighty pounds, "at which my heart was glad, and blessed God." [10] The more regular and legitimate source of income at this period was of course his official salary. When the Diary begins, with the writer filling a minor clerkship, this was fifty pounds a year. After his establishment as Clerk of the Acts, he received three hundred and fifty pounds, and he notes the order which fixed the pay at this figure with much satisfaction. [11]

But in those days, when the distinction between public and private financing was much less critical than at present, such an office as Pepys's meant innumerable opportunities for profit, in addition to the mere wage for official service. The line between legitimate and illegitimate here is naturally very difficult to draw; yet those who have studied Pepys's course with care incline to think that his probity was exceptional for the period in which he lived. We have already observed that he reprehended the taking of direct bribes by others and energetically disclaimed it in his own case. Yet it is pretty to see his conscience waver and tremble in face of an overwhelming temptation: "God forgive me! I found that I could be willing to receive a bribe if it were offered me to conceal my arguments that I found against them." [12] But it does not appear that he did receive it.

And it is one thing to accept a consideration before-

hand for assisting a dubious or even a legitimate trans-
action, another and quite different thing to take a present afterwards for what one has done, or may have
done, out of pure kindness of heart. To the outsider
— who is not making anything — the distinction may
at times seem delicate, and Pepys found it delicate
himself. But he closed his eyes as best he could and
the money somehow came. There is Sir William War-
ren, who gets an advantageous contract for masts, no
doubt a perfectly honest contract, and perfectly good
masts; perhaps better than those of others. And if Sir
William wants to give us a hundred pounds, [13] by all
means take it. There is Mr. Gauden, whom we have
certainly obliged in many ways. A present from him?
Why not? The only trouble is that he has also future
plans in mind that may be affected by our action.
But he assures us that he is thinking only of the past,
and why should we not believe him? "His present,
which hitherto hath been a burden to me, that I could
not do it, because I was doubtfull that he meant it as
a temptation to me to stand by him in the business of
Tangier victualling; but he clears me it was not. . . . .
and that what he did was for my old kindnesses to
him in dispatching of his business, which I was glad
to hear." [14] As any man would be.

But conscience does have to walk a thorny, hubbly

road, undoubtedly. For instance, there are all the complicated transactions in which the State will profit and we can profit at the same time. Why in the name of heaven should we refuse an honest penny that comes in such a fashion as this? Let us admit the case with perfect frankness. There is nothing to be ashamed of in it. That tar question: "Some tarr that I have been endeavouring to buy, for the market begins apace to rise, upon us, and I would be glad first to serve the King well, and if I could I find myself now begin to cast how to get a penny myself." [15] And then there is the complicated affair of the Tangier victualling. If I get it for my contractors and at their price, there is a big bonus in it for me. And I believe in them and in their goods, and their price is a fair one. But, hang it all, there is something about the whole procedure that I don't just like. And sometimes I sigh for that country peace and quiet which I shall never taste. Only, the money does come in, and I do need it sorely, and, well, others are doing things far worse than I would ever do. So we shut our eyes tighter, and embark on that queer business of privateers, in which we first beg a ship from the royal Navy and then, as it were, run a competition with it. But the profit is considerable.

Also, these various persons whom one has obliged

will persist in giving other things besides money, which they are too delicate to offer and suspect that one might be too delicate to take. And it is all very pleasant and nourishes cordiality, after the suggestion of the French proverb. There is Mr. Deane, of Woolwich, "hath sent me the modell he had promised me; but it so far exceeds my expectations, that I am sorry almost he should make such a present to no greater a person." [16] And there are gifts of far more solid value, plate and jewels. Sometimes even they are so costly that one's old Roman virtue rebels and one refuses. Especially is this the case when the object is more likely to appeal to the eye of the lady of the household than to one's own. Thus, when W. Hewer presents a locket of diamonds, worth about forty pounds, Pepys insists peremptorily upon its being returned. "I do not like that she should receive it, it not being honourable for me to do it . . . and she did this evening force him to take it back, at which she says he is troubled; but, however, it becomes me more to refuse it, than to let her accept of it." [17] Yet, on another occasion, Mrs. Pepys is allowed to accept a pair of white gloves, and the husband is undeniably pleased to find forty pieces of good gold enveloped in them.[18] I hope the lady got the gold as well as the gloves. And there are cabinets,[19]

and there are flagons,[20] and altogether the mere perquisites of a Clerk of the Acts must be regarded as a
substantial addition to his capital assets.

Besides these official sources of income, there are
more personal ones, perhaps less open to criticism by
the scrupulous, but hardly more free from vexation
and annoyance. There is the matter of inheritances.
From his father Pepys had not a great deal to expect directly. But, as happens so often, there was at
least the future relief which would be involved in
the old gentleman's decease. "I keep but three men
and a boy yet, till my mother be dead," says Slen-
der, in "The Merry Wives of Windsor"; and Pepys
is equally frank, if with a little more aspect of decorum: "I suppose myself to be worth about £500
clear in the world, and my goods of my house my
own, and what is coming to me from Brampton,
when my father dies, which God defer." [21] The same
bare and terrible frankness appears in many a passage
relating to those cruel strains which the passage of
money from generation to generation is so apt to
entail: "The truth is I am fearful lest my father
should die before debts are paid, and then the land
goes to Tom and the burden of paying all debts will
fall upon the rest of the land. Not that I would do
my brother any real hurt." [22] Certainly not. But,

after all, one has rights, and one's wife has rights, and money is such a vital thing. One must look after it, even if a moderate sacrifice of more sentimental considerations is involved.

When it is a question of collateral inheritances, the ardor is increased and the necessity for displaying sentiment is much diminished. Oh, the cold, harsh, bitter, human truth of such touches as the following: "Waked this morning with news, brought me by a messenger on purpose, that my uncle Robert is dead, and died yesterday; so I rose sorry in some respect, glad in my expectations in another respect. . . . My father and I lay together to-night, I greedy to see the will, but did not ask to see it till to-morrow." [23] Greedy to see the will: the horror, and the veracity!

So living uncles must be conciliated. There is my uncle Wight, an objectionable sort of person, it appears, and much too inclined to be friendly to my wife, in view of her undeniable attraction. He is interested to know if there is any prospect of children. That must mean that he is about to make a will. [24] Why not fool him a little? Where would be the harm? And when uncles die, the question of legacies must be attended to promptly and followed up, and cousins must be interviewed, and journeys must be made. There are witnesses to interrogate and dates to establish and degrees of kin to clarify. And, after all, a prior claim may throw us out and at any rate keep us for days in a tempest of anxiety, perhaps over not so many pounds; but there is the matter of right and the natural unwillingness to be duped and made a fool of. When titles are in doubt, tenants get troublesome and purchasers grow cold.[25] And it may come to the point of actual controversy, which is always so disagreeable. But what can you do? You see it your way, and your cousins see it their way. And why should you give in? So you choose arbitrators, and foolishly choose members of the family: "They began very high in their demands, and my friends, partly being not so well acquainted with the will, and partly, I doubt, not being so good wits as they, for which I blame my choosing of relations (who besides that are equally engaged to stand for them as me), I was much troubled thereat." [26] It may even be dragged into court, which is vexatious and disgraceful, though it is some small comfort that one makes a wonderfully good appearance: "to all which I did give him such answers and spoke so well, and kept him so to it, that all the Court was silent to hear us, and by report since do confess they did never hear the like in the place." [27] But the final outcome of all the trouble is at least a certain increase of our possessions.

II

WHAT counts, however, in the end, is not these outside accretions of income, but the steady habit of saving. If the money is flowing out and leaking out and melting away, what matter how fast it comes in? There can be no permanent accumulation. Therefore you must cultivate thrift. You must watch, you must restrain. Why, the mere appearance of the thing goes a long way. There is Uncle Robert and his project of buying land. By all means join him in it and agree to do a good share. What if I have not the money? Agree, all the same, "that he may think me to be a greater saver than I am." [28] But the reality is of far more consequence than the appearance, is in fact vital, and we must never forget it or lose sight of it. To be sure, there is the danger of miserliness, and the curious truth of human nature, which we note, as we do all such truths, that the more we have, the more we want, and the habit of saving engenders itself: "It is a strange thing to observe and fit for me to remember that I am at no time so unwilling to part with money as when I am concerned in the getting of it most." [29] But, on the other hand, the habit of spending is even more encroaching and dangerous. There is so much that one wants, and it so easy to reach out and get it. And always there is that terrible, vague, dependent future, hanging over us: every penny of saving now is so much protection and insurance against that. So, when the year's outlay is figured up and runs to over a thousand pounds, even though income to a certain extent justifies it, one is rather appalled: "Which is a sum not fit to be said that ever I should spend in one year, before I am master of a better estate than I am." [30]

The true way to save is to use one's imagination a little and think what saving means, or might mean. Especially is this advantageous when appealing to the instinct of thrift in one's wife, who perhaps has not said instinct very highly developed, at any rate in comparison with some others. If we paint a vivid picture of all the luxury and enjoyment she can have in the future, she may be willing to dispense with a few gewgaws in the present: "With my mind much eased talking long in bed with my wife about our frugall life for the time to come, proposing to her what I could and would do if I were worth £2,000, that is, to be a knight, and keep my coach, which pleased her." [31] As it naturally would do; but whether the argument was altogether effective is somewhat open to doubt.

When you have saved your money, the next question that arose, three centuries ago, as to-day, was, what you were to do with it. As the great economist, whom I have before quoted, sagely remarks, "there are ten men who can get property for one who can keep it." And in Pepys's day there was not the luxury of at any rate nominally safe investments offering themselves at every street corner, nor were there savings-banks or elaborate banking facilities of any kind. You could buy land, of course; but then as now buying land meant large certain outlay and small and very dubious income. The unearned increment was perhaps also unheard of. At least it was very slow in coming. Meanwhile tenants grumbled and defaulted and made life a burden, as they do now. You could lend, and sometimes you do it to your own disadvantage, and again you astonish yourself by having the courage to refuse: "I had the unusual wit to deny him." [32] And sometimes there is the prospect of a good return. But we don't know: once let your money out of your hands, and there is no telling when it will come back: "He offering me upon my request to put out some money for me into Backewell's hands at 6 percent interest, which he seldom gives, which I will consider of, being doubtful of trusting any of these great dealers because of their mortality." [33] And then there are speculative ventures of all sorts, chances to risk little and get much, such as have tempted the unwary from the first invention of cash. There is even plain gambling, highly diverting to watch, and seductive, very seductive, especially when accompanied with the assurance that "no man was ever known to lose the first time, the devil being too cunning to discourage a gamester." [34] But Pepys resists, and takes pride in himself for it.

After all, it seems better and safer a good deal of the time to keep the cash in hand, where we can watch it for safety and count it for comfort. We may lend a little to Lord Sandwich, partly for old obligation; but even this is perilous and a mighty cause of anxiety and care. Get the good red gold and have it by us; then we are sure of it, and sure of all the reliance and independence it brings with it: "Lastly, I am providing against a foule day to get as much money into my hands as I can, at least out of the publique hands, that so, if a turne, which I fear, do come, I may have a little to trust to." [35]

The devil of it is that it is risky in such times, or in any times, to have so much cash about. Independence is very well to boast of; but a man who has a few thousand pounds in his back closet is plaguily, dependent, after all. There are thieves: "Now it is

86

strange to think how, knowing that I have a great sum of money in my house, this puts me into a most mighty affright, that for more than two hours, I could not almost tell what to do or say, but feared this and that, and remembered that this evening I saw a woman and two men stand suspiciously in the entry, in the darke." [36] There is fire, which, after the great conflagration, makes wealth and even life seem so strangely uncertain. There are wars and rumours of wars, and when the threat of invasion is upon us, there seems no resource but to send the stuff into the country to be buried in a hole in the ground. This is done by Mr. Pepys senior and Mrs. Pepys, but done so carelessly that it is a cause of endless worry and trouble till it is dug up again, and even then, "I perceive the earth was got among the gold, and wet, so that the bags were all rotten, and all the notes, that I could not tell what in the world to say to it . . . which, all put together, did make me mad." [37] As well it might.

Clearly, great possessions are not always breeders of peace. Yet there is an undeniable charm in seeing them pile up. There is the sense of security, there is the sense of superiority to one's neighbours, there is the sense of being able to purchase what one wishes to, and strange how with this sense comes a certain indifference to such purchasing, as if the ability almost carried with it the satisfaction of the need itself. So that Pepys makes his monthly and yearly summations, with a mighty contentment — when they are on the right side, and when they are not, he resolves to see that they become so: "My monthly accounts, which is now fallen again to £630 or thereabouts, which not long since was £680, at which I am sorry, but I trust in God I shall get it up again, and in the meantime will live sparingly." [38] Then it comes up, and the spirits rise: "I do hope that every day I shall see more and more the pleasure of looking after my business and laying up of money, and blessed be God for what I have already been enabled by his grace to do." [39]

III

BUT besides the getting of money and the keeping of it, there is the spending of it. This would seem to require neither training nor experience, being gracefully inherent in the nature of man. As the comic poet has it:

> "Men have to learn to get, to save, to keep;
> But no man ever had to learn to spend."

Yet even here there is something in habit. If you have grown up poor and seen the shillings come hardly, there is a certain grudging, a certain wonder,

88

about seeing them flit away. And Pepys caught this shade of feeling, as so many others: "emptied a £50 bag, and it was a joy to me to see that I am able to part with such a sum, without much inconvenience; at least, without any trouble of mind." [40]

Still, it is extraordinary how quickly you get into the way of it. There are the things that are necessary, and the things that are pleasant, and the things that are quite superfluous, but which you must have simply because others do, and these are apt to be the most costly and the most profitless of all. There is dress: as time goes on, we have to bestow more and more thought on it. It must be remembered that Pepys lived in a dressing age, when men wore color and rich, expensive ornament, and vied with each other in it, and asserted their position in life by it. There comes a day when he wants to speak to the King about pressing business; "but my linen was so dirty and my clothes mean, that I neither thought it fit to do that, nor go to other persons at the Court, with whom I had business, which did vex me, and I must remedy it." [41] And he does remedy it, since "clothes I perceive more and more every day is a great matter." [42] He buds and blossoms out in fine laces and ruffles and embroidered waistcoats and gaudy coats, and he enjoys them with a child's enjoyment, and tells us so. How charming is the touch about the new watch: "But, Lord! to see how much of my old folly and childishnesse hangs upon me still that I cannot forbear carrying my watch in my hand in the coach all this afternoon, and seeing what o'clock it is one hundred times." [43]

And, although his vanity never takes the form of alluding to it, it is probable that in his stately and well-fitting garments he was a striking and handsome figure of a man. To be sure, the strongly marked features suggest vigor and decision and at most sensuousness, rather than sensibility; but there is a depth and passion in the dark eyes and a dignity in the carriage of the head which must have been impressive.

Dress, however, was a comparatively small item in the expense account. Though one means to be a sober citizen, a staid, hard-working, domestic official, who goes through his round of daily duties, and holds up his head respectably in the community in decency and honesty, it is amazing how many diversions and amusements and entertainments present themselves, and every one of them costs money. The theatre! The theatre is a passion with us. And music! It would seem that music ought not to cost much. But the instruments are expensive, and the lessons are expensive, and when a group of poor musicians has given us pleasure, we cannot refuse them a gratuity. Only we must hasten to set it down in that little account-book: "Had musique whose innocence pleased me, and I did give them 3s." [44] Then, if you are interested in scientific matters, there is the expense of curious experiments, and if you need instruments, of course the best makers must make them, and the charge is high. Food costs money, and drink costs money, and journeying costs money. Friends cost money, and perhaps one spends even more on those who are not friends, but must be treated as if they were. Ah, it is an extravagant world. The whole ten years of the Diary are the record of a battle between the instinct of outlay for delight and the instinct of saving for protection. Would not your diary and mine be much the same? And desperate measures have sometimes to be resorted to. There is that strange business of vows, which will have to be looked into later, and which perhaps would not be so strange, if it were possible to read all men's hearts. And then again we defy prudence and caution altogether. This is our day and we should enjoy it: "Though I am much against too much spending, yet I do think it best to enjoy some degree of pleasure now that we have health, money, and opportunity, rather than to leave pleasures to old age and poverty, when we cannot have them so properly." [45]

And so to consider the various phases of outlay more in detail. There is the buying of books. Pepys had much of the collector's instinct and passion, and his love for the purchase of books resulted in the noble library which has borne his name for two hundred years. He liked the rare and curious, as the collector does, liked to be the acquirer and possessor of something which the rest of the world did not have and could not get. He mentions with delight the discovery of a "History of the Turkish Policy," for which he paid fifty-five shillings, when it might have been bought before the great fire for twenty. But he adds that there are only six copies, of which two went to the King and the Duke of York. [46] He has those splendid bursts of pride over a temptation resisted, when one looks and longs and even touches, and then goes away without buying anything. "Whence I walked home, calling a little in Paul's Churchyard, and, I thank God, can read and never buy a book, though I have a great mind to it." [47] He has those struggles, when one debates and doubts, makes up one's mind and unmakes it again, as we see in Professor Child's charming dealings with the rose catalogues: "I took to reading a rose catalogue, which resulted in my ordering more roses, which resulted in remorse, which resulted in my tearing up the order." [48] So Pepys; only his remorse comes too late: "So to a picture-seller's by the Half Moone in the street over against the Exchange, and there looked over the maps of several cities and did buy two books of cities stitched together cost me 9s. 6d., and when I came home thought of my vowe, and paid 5s. into my poor box for it, hoping in God that I shall forfeit no more in that kind." [49] But he did, all the same, and books and pictures grew to be more of a temptation and luxury, as the habit of such things is.

And there is the necessary domestic outlay, less seductive and picturesque, but more constant and draining. The house you live in has to be made and kept habitable, even if it does not belong to you, and alterations cost money, and also drag and wear and fret and consume an undue portion of life. You get your rooms done over, and then the rain comes and upsets everything: "Found all my ceilings spoiled with rain last night, so that I fear they must be all new whited when the work is done." [50] You try to attend to other matters, but this home upheaval is too absorbing: you cannot keep away from it, or let it alone: "My mind is so set upon these things that I cannot but be with the workmen to see things done to my mind, which if I am not there is seldom done." [51] And you conclude with a bit of wonder at what is perhaps not so wonderful, if you take the experience of humanity at large: "And strange it is to think how building do fill my mind and put out all other things out of my thoughts." [52]

When your house is altered to suit you, if it ever is, you have to furnish it, and the expense here is deadly because it is so much a matter of mere renewal. New books and new pictures carry their excitement with them. But worn-out linen has to be replaced by other linen, which will wear out too soon. Dishes break in the most injudicious and disconcerting manner. Furniture gets old and rickety: to repair it is troublesome and costs as much as to buy new. And the neat little sum that you had set apart for pleasures or for emergencies is quickly consumed in these quite unexpected and as it seems quite unnecessary vexations. "My wife came home having been abroad today, laying out above £12 in linen, and a copper, and pot and bedstead, and other household stuff, which troubles me also, so that my mind to-night is very heavy and divided." [53] Furthermore, do the best you can, you are tempted by bits of ornament, trifles, baubles, that serve no particular purpose, but glitter and may perhaps be bought cheap: "The first thing like a bawble I have bought a good while, but I do it with some trouble of mind." [54] Yet in the end you get things about you that are decent and comfortable and it is worth the money when you pay a visit to those wretched Penns and come back and congratulate yourself: "Home to supper and to bed, talking with my wife of the poorness and meanness of all that Sir W. Pen and the people about us do, compared with what we do." [55]

Then there are the servants, another unfailing and not altogether satisfactory occasion of outlay. In the early days, when Mrs. Pepys does the work, there is more comfort and quiet, after all. But the mistress of the household, as well as the master, must have leisure to enjoy herself, and we must entertain, and to do it suitably it is necessary to have more hands, and then it is necessary to pay them. And heaven knows, the pay is little enough compared to what is paid in America in the twentieth century, a few pounds a year and board for hard and incessant work. Yet, little as it is, it is agitating, and one debates a long while and finally decides with many qualms as to possible unforeseen outlay which such indulgence may entail. Even when the proposed maid has manifest recommendations and good qualities, there is the doubt: "I fear greater inconveniences of expenses, and my wife's liberty will follow, which I must study to avoid till I have a better purse." [56] But one's position in the world does demand a certain amount of display. There is a scale of appearances, and a Clerk of the Acts, with a good salary and perquisites, must go attended in a manner to do credit to his office and his employers: "Our boy waiting on us with his sword, which this day he begins to wear, to outdo Sir W. Pen's boy, who this day, and Sir W. Batten's too, begin to wear new livery; but I do take mine to be the neatest of them all." [57]

The same considerations apply to the table. Though we like good things well enough, we can be contented with simple fare for ourselves, live sparingly and save here also. But a guest may arrive at any time, and we must be ready to do honour to him. And then in the old days the belly was pinched so often that it is pleasant to make up for it, now one can. There was that February afternoon in '62 when I ran across friends dining and would fain have eaten freely, but "I ate some bread and butter, having ate nothing all day, while they were by chance discoursing of Marriot, the great eater, so that I was, I remember, ashamed to eat what I would have done." [58] But that is gone and past now, and we have all the luxuries of the season. No matter who may drop in, even Sir W. Penn, we are ready for him, and can serve him such a meal that there will be nothing to be ashamed of.

Why, for only just my wife and me there are dainties that would be fit for the king: "At noon a good venison pasty and a turkey to ourselves without any body so much as invited by us, a thing unusuall for so small a family of my condition: but we did it, and were very merry." [59]

So much for indoors. And outdoors there is the coach. Oh, that coach! What a subject of discussion and anxiety and controversy! Impossible to think of such a thing till a secure accumulation of capital permits and justifies it. Yet the Penns flaunt about so insolently in theirs! And it is really such a disgrace to have to depend upon hackney-coaches, so dilatory and so dirty, though, to be sure, there was a day when a pair of sturdy English legs served all purposes well enough. But one has other uses for them now. And the hackney-coach is simply impossible: "Thence, in the evening, with my people in a glass hackney coach to the park, but was ashamed to be seen." [60] So the land for a coach-house is bought, after much argument, and the coach is selected, after much comparison and bargaining. And then one rides in it. But, oh, the downfall of human hopes! See what happens:

> "The glories of our blood and state
> Are shadows, not substantial things."

"We set out, out of humour — I because Betty, whom I expected, was not come to go with us; and my wife that I would sit on the same seat with her which she likes not, being so fine: and she then expected to meet Sheres, which we did in the Pell Mell, and, against my will, I was forced to take him into the coach, but was sullen all day almost, and little complaisant: the day also being unpleasing, though the Park full of coaches, but dusty and windy, and cold, and now and then a little dribbling rain; and, what made it worst, there were so many hackney-coaches as spoiled the sight of the gentlemens'; and so we had little pleasure." [61] Alas, alas!

It will be noted that there was another spending power in the Pepys establishment, besides the husband. The financial aspect of Mrs. Pepys's existence will call for consideration later, in connection with her personal outlay. Meantime it must be remembered that the domestic expenditure had to be carried on largely through her, and this necessarily involved placing greater or less amounts of money in her hands. She had nothing of her own, and never expected to have. She was a child when she was married and had never had the management of funds, nor understood anything about them. It does not appear that her husband gave her any specific allowance, or attempted more than a rather hand-to-mouth financial procedure. Perhaps it would have been difficult to do otherwise. Under the circumstances, relations were no more strained than might have been expected. Pepys was fairly, if spasmodically, liberal, and I have no doubt Mrs. Pepys did her loyal best. Yet when she frankly and cheerfully confesses that she falsifies her accounts, the husband is driven nearly to frenzy.[62] And at another time, a deficit of seven shillings induces a highly painful scene: "I indeed too angrily insisting upon so poor a thing, and did give her very provoking high words, calling her beggar, and reproaching her friends, which she took very stomachfully and reproached me justly with mine, and I confess, being myself, I cannot see what she could have done less." [63] But what a thing a diary is for exposing the soul, at least when you keep it as this man did!

IV

FINALLY, after the chapters of getting and saving, we come to that of giving, and it must be admitted that with Pepys this is briefer than the others. Would not the same be true of a good many of us?

To begin with, there were the needs of his relatives, which constitute such a considerable element in the budget of most men who are making their own way in the world. There were father and mother Pepys. We are to suppose that they had made some sacrifices in getting Samuel started on his upward career, and Samuel is ready, if not eager, to recognize the obligation. Mr. Pepys senior had an income of his own, but hardly enough to keep him in comfort. On one occasion his son gives him money to buy him a horse, and distributes various sums among the ladies of the family for the purchase of little necessaries and luxuries.[64] On other occasions the supply afforded is more substantial. And the son, as I said, is ready enough, cordial enough, acknowledges all he owes to the parental care. Yet any dependence is galling, and I doubt if I should have liked to be dependent upon the charity of Samuel Pepys. I doubt if his father liked it, either: "I find his spending hitherto has been (without extraordinary charges) at full £100 per annum, which troubles me, and I did let him apprehend it, so as that the poor man wept, though he did make it well appear to me that he could not have saved a farthing of it."[65] An unpleasant scene, but no doubt often repeated in human history. As to the mother, the following delicious spiritual jumble gives an idea of the final cost of disposing of her: "Vexed at two or three things, viz: that my wife's watch proves so bad as it do; the ill

state of the office; and Kingdom's business; at the
charge which my mother's death for mourning will
bring me when all paid." [66]

Then there is brother Tom who considers marriage.
And it seems to be patently a matter of bargain and
sale. Various young women are debated; but they do
not bring enough or they demand too much, and the
whole matter entails endless vexation. Later brother
Tom dies, and his estate has to be looked after, which
seems to mean principally that his creditors have to
be paid. Also, brother John has to be educated for the
Church, at somebody's expense. And there is sister
Paulina (Pall), whose conduct and character are not
in all respects approved by her critical brother; but
for the sake of getting her well married he is willing to
pay, and liberally, even being beguiled into relinquish-
ing what he had prudently reserved: "My cozen had
got me to give the odd sixth £100 presently, which I
intended to keep to the birth of the first child: and let
it go — I shall be eased of the care." [67]

Further, there are Mrs. Pepys's relatives to be provided for, since they seem little able to do for themselves. It is to Pepys's credit that he continued this
helpfulness long after his wife's death. But there is
always the same grudge, which money fatally begets,
which so many feel and so few acknowledge. "My

wife this day hears from her father and mother . . . he, poor good man! I think he is, gives her good counsel still, which I always observed of him, and thankful for my small charities to him. I could be willing to do something for them, were I sure not to bring them over again hither." [68]

With broader benevolences of a private and individual order the Diary does not abound. Pepys's incurable taste for playing the grand signor does indeed produce occasional indiscriminate largess: "The poor, as they did yesterday, did stand at the coach to have something given them, as they do to all great persons; and I did give them something: and the town musique did also come and play: but, Lord! what sad music they made!" [69] Yet, feeling sure, as we do, that anything in the form of elaborate giving would have found its significant place in those all-recording pages, one rather wonders to hear no more of it. And, on the contrary, the eternal human avoidance of those who would beg or borrow is never overlooked. "But to see how apt every man is to forget friendship in time of adversity. How glad was I when he was gone, for fear he should ask me to be bond for him, or to borrow money of me." [70] Still, we should not forget how notable and penetrating this constant candor is. Perhaps, after making all due allowance for it, we might

discover that Pepys was quite as ready, as well as unready, to give as the rest of the world. At any rate, we
should recognize the equal, charming sincerity of an
admission in a somewhat different tone: "I pity her,
and will do her what kindness I can: yet I observe
something of ill-nature in myself more than should be,
that I am colder towards her in my charity than I
should be to one so painful as he and she have been
and full of kindness to their power to my wife and
I." [71] Also, we should remember those fines and for-
feits which were perpetually going into the poor-box.
They were paid in with regret, but they must have
been paid out with benefit to somebody.

The matter of public gifts and charities one would
think might have made a considerable appeal to
Pepys, inasmuch as his vanity would have been grati-
fied as well as his instinct of human kindness. But during the period of the Diary, at any rate, he was too en-
grossed with his own affairs and his official duties to
have much thought for large philanthropy. In later
years ampler leisure and more abundant means evidently inclined him more to dwell upon the needs of
others and there are indications of his being gener-
ously disposed towards both religion and education.
Moreover, the tone in which Pepys's contemporaries
speak of him implies a man of liberal and kindly

nature, who was ready to do his full share in carrying on the good causes of the world.

And, for all his thought and all his thrift, Pepys does not seem to have left a large property behind him. His will disposes of considerable sums, but these legacies were contingent upon the payment of a large amount due from the Crown, which was never collected. We may, therefore, feel that he got the good of his wealth, both in spending and in giving. As Evelyn so admirably expresses it: "O *fortunate* Mr. Pepys! who knows, possesses, and enjoys all that is worth seeking after." [72] In what concerns money, at any rate, it may justly be said that he was a shrewd, practical, reasonable, liberal man of the world.

IV
PEPYS AND HUMANITY

I

PEPYS brings to the portrayal of his manifold general relations with humanity the same infinite straightforwardness that he applies to all his dealings with every aspect of life and death.

And first, he delighted in the various phases and manifestations of human intercourse and activity. He was never tired of watching men live, make their strange, unaccountable gestures, go through their merry, or dreary, or passionate antics, and then settle quietly down into the grave. All men were pretty much the same to him, from this point of view, the farmer, the shepherd, the sailor, the soldier, the merchant, the preacher, the actor, the gambler, all afforded him entertainment and curious matter for dry, sincere, depicting comment, which would give them a far longer life than they enjoyed in this world. He liked travel, made caustic and vivid notes on his journeys. No matter how tired his legs might be, his eyes were keen. Whether in Brampton or in Tangier, he was always on the watch: rugged, homely English peasants and draped, melodramatic Moors, all alike were game for him. He must have been a delightful travelling companion, if the fleas and the fees and the delays and the bad food did not fret him too much: they may have.

Anyway, there was matter enough right at home, in the parks and the back streets and the public places of London, to satisfy even his almost insatiable curiosity. And always, on every figure and every little incident that crops up about him, there is some odd, suggestive, startling observation, which leaves them unforgettable. Sometimes the comment is a mere quick sketching, which makes things stand out, and you cannot tell how. Sometimes it rises to great heights of interpretative power. Take the graveyard scene and the civil grave-digger, who might have stepped right out of "Hamlet": "He would, for my father's sake do my brother that is dead all the civility he can; which was to disturb other corps that are not quite rotten, to make room for him; and methought his manner of speaking it was very remarkable; as of a thing that now was in his power to do a man a courtesy or not." [1]

It is to be noted that in all this vast presentation of the surface of life, which would seem to afford so much of humorous contrast and comic diversion, Pepys almost never succeeds in making the reader laugh with

SAMUEL PEPYS

Portrait by Sir Peter Lely

him, and does not very often attempt it. Whether it
be partly in the spirit of Emerson's remark, which I
have quoted, that jokes do not easily get into the
diary-soliloquy, or whether the man himself lacked
the ironic turn that Lamb or Mark Twain must have
given to a diary or anything else, it is difficult to say.
In actual talk Pepys might have made you laugh
freely when he laughed. As a writer of diary you often
smile good-naturedly at him, but you do not take him
for a humorist. It is true that he himself sometimes
laughs loud and long; but you read the account of it,
and, though you sympathize, you are hardly overcome. There are the snorers: "Lord! the mirth which
it caused me to be waked in the night by their snoaring round about me; I did laugh till I was ready to
burst, and waked one of the two companions of Tem-
ple, who could not a good while tell where he was
that he heard one laugh so, till he recollected himself,
and I told him what it was at, and so to sleep again,
they still snoaring." [2] And there are his occasional
practical jokes, like the farce in connection with the
stealing of Sir William Penn's tankard,[3] or the pleasant jest of the swearing boys: "I had the sport to see
two boys swear, and stamp, and fret, for not being
able to get their horse over a stile and ditch, one of
them swearing and cursing most bitterly; and I would

fain in revenge, have persuaded him to have drove his horse through the ditch, by which I believe he would have stuck there. But the horse would not be drove, and so they were forced to go back again, and so I walked away homeward." [4] All which is not unamusing, but belongs to a rather elementary type of fun.

Also it is somewhat suggestive of ill-nature, like a good many practical jokes; yet Pepys was not ill-natured: he only saw life and took it as it came. Indeed, he had his marked share of human sensibility, quick and ready response to the emotions of those about him, sympathetic understanding and kindly appreciation. When he sees people happy, he enjoys it, sometimes, to be sure, with a frankly admitted trace of envy, sometimes with a suggestion that they are making a good deal of little things; but he enjoys it, all the same. When he sees people suffering, it agitates him, disturbs him, even distresses him, and he makes moderate efforts to relieve them. How many persons make more?

He is sensitive to human sorrow in general, keenly aware of the large and haunting misery of our mortal lot. The sight of a murdered man makes the Diary even more indecipherable than usual: "a sad spectacle, and a broad wound, which makes my hand now shake to write of it." [5] The memory of a dead body left floating upon the Thames for four days, with no one bothering to take it out, proves strangely troubling.[6] The melancholy story of the mistress of the Beare Tavern, who drowned herself, excites dismal reflections, much augmented by her having been "a most beautiful woman, as most I have seen." [7]

And he has direct social sympathy, puts himself in other people's places, feels the awkwardness of a domestic situation more, perhaps, than the actors themselves. When a lady whom he is visiting scolds her husband, Pepys hardly knows which way to look: She "did speak very discontented and angry to the Captain for disappointing a gentleman that he had invited to dinner, which he took like a wise man and said little, but she was very angry, which put me clear out of countenance that I was sorry I went in." [8] Or, take the much deeper note in the charming scene with the old woman in the country, surprised by the arrival of the young girl she loved: "Where comes in another poor woman, who, hearing that Deb was here, did come running hither, and with her eyes so full of tears, and heart so full of joy, that she could not speak when she come in, that it made me weep too: I protest that I was not able to speak to her, which I would have done, to have diverted her tears." [9] Nor was the sympathy confined to mere emotion. At his own time and in his own way Pepys could and did give sensible advice and intelligent assistance, tempered always with the consideration of his own ability, which must be weighed and duly noted in the record, like everything else.

But what is most attractive about Pepys's sympathy, and what is perhaps also somewhat in advance of his time, is his tenderness and consideration for animals. He seems to have been fond of pets, to have watched them, and fostered them, and cherished them. And, with the true instinct in such things, he clings to the old and cannot get used to the new. He is much troubled to hear that the canary bird, which he has had for three or four years, is dead.[10] On the other hand, when his wife is presented with a mighty pretty spaniel, "as a new comer, I cannot be fond of her."[11] Suffering, or ill-treatment, of dumb creatures irritates and distresses him. When he finds a son of Sir Heneage Finch beating a poor dog to death, "it makes him mad to see it."[12] When his own pet is in trouble, it is equally disturbing: "I bethought myself that we had left our poor little dog that followed us out of doors at the waterside, and God knows whether he be not lost, which did not only strike my wife into a great passion but I must confess myself also; more than was becoming me."[13]

The same elements of kindness, combined in due proportion with irritability and imperiousness, appear in Pepys's relations with the series of domestic servants whose coming and going is chronicled in his pages. The amorous side of these relations will claim its place in a later chapter of this study. But there were other sides in plenty; and as the long and variegated train of boys and maids files before us, we begin to feel that few things better exhibit fundamental traits than a man's — or woman's — dealing with those who make his daily existence tolerable — or intolerable.

It is evident that Pepys believed in family discipline. These boys were put into his hands partly for his convenience, partly also for their own good. Strict and rigorous measures were absolutely necessary, if he was to get his service out of them, and incidentally, if their souls were to be saved. He reasons and remonstrates, points out the way that should be followed. If they do not choose to follow, there is a rod ready, and energetic arms waiting to apply it. The boy tells a lie. The lie is brought home to him, so that he cannot possibly deny it, or explain it. Whereupon the master beats him thoroughly: "I did extremely beat him, and though it did trouble me to do it, yet I thought it necessary to do it." [14] The same thing happens again; only the master frankly confesses that the rods were so small that the castigating arm was considerably more damaged than the boy.[15] And on another occasion we wonder whether the same circumstance may not serve to explain the master's puzzle, "that such a little boy as he could possibly be able to suffer half so much as he did to maintain a lie. . . . So to bed with my arm very weary." [16]

And there were times when temper as well as discipline entered into the case. There was that mortifying kick administered to Luce, our cook-mayde, doubly mortifying because it was seen "by Sir W. Pen's foot-boy, which did vex me to the heart, because I know he will be telling their family of it; though I did put on presently a very pleasant face to the boy, and spoke kindly to him, as one without passion, so as it may be he might not think I was angry." [17]

Yet there was also much genuine, sweet, normal affection in these domestic relations. There was dependence and counsel and even pleasant and profitable talk at suitable times. Here, as with the pets, it is clear that Pepys was loyal, got attached to persons and faces, clung to them, hated to part from them and was glad to see them return. When "poor Jane, my old, little Jane," comes to us again, we are greatly contented.[18] When we are obliged to dismiss one who has served us long and well, the tears are very near flowing,[19] and this not on one occasion only, but on several, so closely do these humble but essential ministers of comfort twine themselves into our lives.

II

PEPYS's dealings with the different members of his family are of constant interest and importance to his readers. We have already considered the financial aspect of these, but this is comparatively secondary. No one realized more fully than he, though perhaps he does not definitely analyze it, the clinging quality of the blood-relationships. Our friends are bound to us by links of sympathy which are too apt to change with age, so that the friendships wither and leave us. Our blood connections are often less warm, because such sympathy does not enter into them, but they last; and even, with the fading of friendship, they are apt to acquire more strength. As the years pass, uncles and cousins, though fairly distant and though at times subject to suspicion and controversy over little questions of inheritance, seem somehow to become more and more part of ourselves.

In what is usually the closest blood-relation of all, Pepys is not particularly impressive. We get very little glimpse of his childish dependence upon and affection for his mother, and during the diary period she appears as rather fretful and querulous, not perhaps actually broken, but certainly not active and efficient. Her son does indeed refer with sadness to leaving her, when he feared he might never see her again.[20] But too often he is led to speak of her, and even to her, with a touch of acrimony. She is "unsufferably foolish and simple,"[21] he declares, and those who have to make their country home with her occasionally find her trying. Pepys remonstrates with her on the economical quality of her table,[22] which seems a little hard, considering that it is all saving to him. He is obliged to snub her in her appeal in behalf of a younger brother's waywardness, though he endeavors to do it in kind words.[23] Above all, she is too disposed to friction with her husband, as about the maid, "which my father likes and my mother dislikes."[24] The son feels bound to lecture on all these topics. He urges patience and tolerance with the father, he preaches good housekeeping, and then admonishes most decidedly against the tendency to extravagance, "which I did to make her leave off her spending, which I find she is now-a-days very free in, building upon what is left to us by my uncle to bear her out in it, which troubles me much."[25]

Then the mother dies, and the approach of death, as is the remorseless habit of it, brings up old memories and strange forgotten tenderness; and the haunting presence of the one we loved and slighted, though it fades in the pressure of daily business, comes back upon us with burning intensity in the solitude of night: "Much troubled in my sleep of my being crying by my mother's bedside, laying my head over hers and crying, she almost dead and dying, and so waked, but what is strange, methought she had hair over her face, and not the same kind of face as my mother really hath, but yet did not consider that, but did weep over her as my mother, whose soul God have mercy of." [26] Can you render better the distortion, the obsession, the terror of dreams? Yet we have, after all, a practical mind, and when the final word comes, though I weep and my wife weeps, I console myself with pointing out to her how much better it is that my mother should die now than survive my father and me and be thrown dependent upon the harsh world: "So to my tailor's, and up and down, and then home and to my office a little, and then to supper and to bed, my heart sad and afflicted, though my judgment at ease." [27] The exquisite aptness of the distinction! And the strange, swift, deadening, protecting current of daily life!

With his father Pepys's tone is constantly quite different from that in which he alludes to his mother. There is, indeed, a shade of patronage, which, taken in connection with the financial support, does not seem wholly compatible with the finest delicacy of feeling. Yet there is such delicacy in the comment about the old shoes: "This day, not for want, but for good husbandry, I sent my father, by his desire, six pair of my old shoes, which fit him, and are good; yet, methought, it was a thing against my mind to have him wear my old things." [28] At times, as with his mother, the son lets himself go to actual reprehension; for example, in the case of father Pepys's letter to cousin Roger on business matters, a reprehension which, the son hopes, will "make him the more carefull to trust to my advice for the time to come without so many needless complaints and jealousys, which are troublesome to me because without reason." [29] This sort of thing is distressing, when you realize that if the financial dependence were the other way, the son would never express himself in such a style. And the same offensive lofty tone is adopted in lecturing the old gentleman as to his domestic affairs and the management of his servants. [30]

Yet it is clear enough that there was enduring sympathy, comfort, confidence between the two. Pepys goes down into the country to visit his father, discusses business with him, travels about with him, shares his room, confers with him on all important matters, and recognizes the value of his judgment and experience. The father comes to London, and the son wants to have him come, looks forward to his coming, and hopes it will revive his spirits and relieve him from something of the drag of domestic infelicity. When he is taken suddenly ill, everything is done to make him comfortable, and the son can scarce forbear weeping at the sight of his distress.[31] When he returns home, he is missed and regretted, and the regret is expressed in terms, which, if a trifle condescending, are by no means without charm: "It rejoices my heart that I am in condition to do anything to comfort him, and could, were it not for my mother, have been contented he should have stayed always here with me, he is such innocent company." [32]

Then there is brother Tom, whose marriage causes Samuel so much anxiety. Whether because his own wife had beauty but no property and was married in youth and haste, with some moments of repentance afterwards, or for whatever reason, the elder brother does not propose to have Thomas's affairs settled without due deliberation. Worldly goods must be looked into and all other circumstances must be considered and weighed before the final decision is adopted. And, as so often happens, too great caution spoils the whole project, all the successive projects, and Tom is left to conclude his not too reputable existence a hopeless bachelor. On his illness and death the Diary is priceless, as on death always. Pepys frequents the bedside with fraternal solicitude and also with a clear vision of the various difficulties and vexations involved in the prospective decease. He avoids the death-chamber, when actual dissolution is imminent, having no mind to see his brother die, but returns immediately after and gives a somewhat gruesome account of the process of laying out, as practised in the seventeenth century.[33] He describes his brother's state of mind when the last hour was approaching and sets down his dying words, with the fretted comment that "this was all the sense, good or bad, that I could get out of him this day." [34] Then he goes home and snuggles up close to his wife, yet confesses "being full of disorder and grief for my brother that I could not sleep nor wake with satisfaction." [35]

And then comes the final comment on the funeral, a comment whose direct, bare horror of commonplace oblivion has not been surpassed by Pepys or any one else: "But, Lord! to see how the world makes nothing of the memory of a man, an houre after he is dead!

And, indeed, I must blame myself; for though at the sight of him dead and dying, I had real grief for a while, while he was in my sight, yet presently after, and ever since, I have had very little grief indeed for him." [36]

As for brother John, since, like his father, he was fortunate enough to live beyond the range of the Diary record, he is saved from such another unceremonious epitaph. It is evident that Samuel tried to do his duty by him, giving not only financial assistance, but good and intelligent advice when it was needed. Perhaps the advice was not always desired, or digested. John was young and wayward, did not greatly care for his elder brother's airs, and wrote letters to Tom not wholly favorable to Sam's lofty pretensions. The letters turned up after Tom's death and caused hard feeling.[37] Also, Samuel cannot get up any great enthusiasm over his brother's vocation as a preacher. Probably he finds it incompatible with some memories of childhood. When John is invited to say grace, he makes but an ill business of it.[38] When his mentor examines his intellectual qualifications, he appears lamentably deficient; "for I do not see that he minds optickes or mathematiques of any sort, nor anything else that I can find." [39]

Yet, after all, a brother is a brother. John has a

sudden, violent attack of illness, "and he was fallen down all along upon the ground, dead, which did put me into a great fright; and, to see my brotherly love! I did presently lift him up from the ground, he being as pale as death. . . . I never was so frighted but once, when my wife was ill at Ware upon the road, and I did continue trembling a good while and ready to weepe to see him." [40] Which induces a certain renewal of affection, together with a train of thought that tends distinctly to the development of family feeling: "My wife loves him mightily as one that is pretty harmless, and I do begin to fancy him from yesterday's accident, it troubling me to think that I should be left without a brother or sister, which is the first time that ever I had thoughts of that kind in my life." [41]

As for the sister, Paulina, it cannot be said that she was ever a source of much solace or satisfaction. At a very early stage of the Diary she is registered as ill-natured and regard for her is imperilled because she is "so cruel a hypocrite that she can cry when she pleases." [42] She shows a deplorable disregard for minor distinctions of *meum* and *tuum*, appropriating Mrs. Pepys's scissors and the maid's book with shameless indifference.[43] Pepys has her up to London, to assist in his domestic economy. This is done with the explicit understanding that she is to be a servant, and only a servant,[44] to which she agrees with humility and gratitude, London probably representing the acme of her dreams. Further, the menial position is emphasized by the absolute refusal to let her sit at table with the family.[45] Under these conditions perhaps it was not strange that the experiment should fail and Pall be relegated in disgrace to the country.

Her brother does not forget her, however, and, as the years go on, realizing that she "grows old and ugly," [46] as he expresses it, he finally arranges a match for her. "I take her to be so cunning and ill-natured, that I have no great love for her; but only she is my sister, and must be provided for." [47] Now I would give a good deal to know what Mr. Jackson, whom she married, thought. At any rate, her second son, John, became her brother's great favorite and heir.

It will be easily understood that all these family relations were much complicated, as they so often are, by the matrimonial element. Mrs. Pepys did not always get on happily with her husband's kin, not with any of them, unless perhaps the erratic, clerical John. I imagine she tried to do so; but she was young, she lived in the London atmosphere, and had lived abroad; she had a keen eye for the fashions and the follies of the world. The Pepys family mainly lived in the country and always savoured of it. So that to keep down bitter feeling between the different elements was not the least of Pepys's difficulties. He appeals now to one, now to the other, not always with perfect success. He represents to the Pepys how important it is that they should conciliate the lady. "Not that I would ever be led by her to forget or desert them in the main, but yet she deserves to be pleased and complied with a little." [48] Entire harmony seems to have been beyond even his power to establish.

Then there are Mrs. Pepys's relatives, who are usually unobjectionable and can be kept at a distance, but do occasionally cause some solicitude. When her father seems at the point of death, Pepys has his priceless mortuary comment: "Which, God forgive me! did not trouble me so much as it should, though I was indeed sorry for it." [49] The mother was harmless, and lived for many years, and was always appreciative of what her son-in-law did for her. Pepys was helpful to the brother Balty (Balthazar) and the helpfulness was acknowledged. But note the exquisite mixture of feelings in the following observation on the nature of the help: "My wife's brother, whom I sent for to offer making him a Muster-Master and send to sea, which the poore man likes well of and will go, and it will be a good preferment to him, only hazardous"![50]

III

FROM the narrower circle of Pepys's family relations we pass to his extensive contact with humanity at large. Among the vast numbers of men he was obliged to meet and deal with, socially as well as officially, there were many who were mere indifferent shapes and shadows, going and coming, many whom he liked and enjoyed, some also naturally whom he disliked and who, perhaps causelessly, inspired ill-feeling and disgust. It must at once be recognized that with these Pepys was inclined to keep his irritation to himself. It was a fighting age, and he carried a sword. He may have had some theoretical experience in using it. But he was by nature a man of peace, and tempers of that kind avoid quarrels with surprising facility and agility.

I fancy that Pepys, in courage as in so many other things, was an average human being. But here, as always, we must remember the candor, perhaps here even more than usual; for the average man does not usually confess his tremors, and a good argument may be made to show that confession tends much to augment them. Pepys confessed them, at any rate, noted them with absolute indifference and sincerity, at times almost seems to gloat over them, with something of the curious satisfaction which they afford his readers.

There is mere imaginative fear in general, fear of spaces and solitude and the dark, such as overcomes the Diarist when he ventures at night into a vast ruin of fortification on Salisbury plain.[51] There was the adventure of the young gibb-cat, which "did leap down our stairs from top to bottom, at two leaps, and frighted us, that we could not tell well whether it was the cat or a spirit, and do sometimes think this morning that the house might be haunted." [52] There is the more concrete fear of thieves, which keeps him shaking half the night when he has treasure in the house and makes him well apprehend the timorous life of the over-greedy rich.[53]

Yet, as regards these more abstract dangers, Pepys had his courage too, and we must not forget his quiet persistence in duty when the plague threatened far more imminent disaster than gibb-cats, or thieves.

As to human friction, the Diarist does not hesitate to reiterate his dislike of it. Let others quarrel and bluster, if they will. Let Sir William Penn knock a couple of ruffians off their horses and be proud of it.[54]

Such proceedings fill us with a certain disgust. To be sure, we can swagger on instinct, when impulse gets the better of us. When we are roused too suddenly from sleep, we can seize a suspected thief by the shoulder: "But when I waked I found my cowardly heart to discover a fear within me and that I should never have done it if I had been awake." [55] Also, there is the delightful incident of the street set-to: "So I being called, went thither, and the fellow coming out again of a shop, I did give him a good cuff or two on the chops, and seeing him not oppose me, I did give him another." [56] Does it not remind you of the charming bit in "A King and No King," when the citizen's wife says to her damaged retainer, "Why did he strike thee, Philip?" and Philip replies, "Because I leaned against him." "And why didst thou lean against him?" "Because I did not think he would have struck me." [57]

Yet even in that age of quick and susceptible honor there is not the slightest indication that people made fun of Pepys's timidity or despised him for it or were aware of it. Without indulging in Rosalind's "swashing and martial outside," I fancy he kept up a good semblance of manly dignity, as we have indeed seen in his relations with his office-mates. And I feel sure that the resentment he so simply and honestly ex-

presses over the ill-treatment of two ladies quite un-
known to him would have impelled him to act not
unnobly when occasion called for it: "I was troubled
to see them abused so; and could have found in my
heart, as little desire of fighting as I have, to have
protected the ladies." [58]

Still, it must be admitted that Pepys is more winning, if not more instructive, in friendly relations
than in hostile. It does not appear that he was
closely intimate with any one. Perhaps the extraordinary frankness of the confidences offered to us
through the Diary would make any mere oral intercourse seem tame and remote. Perhaps the Diary
took the place of friendship to Pepys himself. It may
well have done so. But he knew an immense variety
of men and women, knew them and liked them, and
they apparently liked him, and he exhibits his connection with them at all points with his usual clinging and telling veracity.

On the whole, his attitude to his social, as to his
official, superiors, is satisfactory. Certainly he does
like to get up in the world, to establish and assert his
position, to take steps and do deeds and say words
that will accomplish this end. Who will blame him?
Before you criticize him too closely in detail, you
might do well to consider some things you have done

yourself. If Lord Chancellor Clarendon is disposed
to find fault with him, he is anxiously apologetic and
conciliatory.[59] He goes so far, with Sir William
Coventry, as to desire "he would do the last act of
friendship in telling me of my faults." [60] Which I
hope and believe Sir William was wise enough not to
do, such a performance being apt to be the last act
of friendship indeed. He informs us with the utmost
coolness of the pretence he maintained to forward his
standing in society: "Which is a great pleasure to me
again, to talk with persons of quality, ... and I give
it out among them that the estate left me is £200 a
year in land, besides moneys, because I would put an
esteem upon myself." [61]

Yet, through it all, one gets an impression of dignity and independence, of proper and becoming deference and respect, yet accompanied with the recog-
nition and assertion of substantial worth and manli-
ness on one's own part, which is not to be disregarded
or put down by the insolence of the great. Especially
does Pepys appear well in his relations with his patron
and relative Lord Sandwich. The Earl had made him
all he was in the world and he admits it freely and is
grateful. But he is not going to truckle or be played
with. He will submit to unrewarded toil, will work
hard and make sacrifices at his friend's behest. But

he will not be neglected or maltreated. Also, when he sees the Earl making mistakes, he does not hesitate to point them out, to lament his vices and deplore his follies. He gives respectful advice, which is not only well meant but well worded and deserves to be and is well received. When there is a temporary estrangement, his comment upon it is admirable in tone, could not be bettered, and is in itself sufficient to make one esteem and like him: "However, I am resolved . . . by grave and humble, though high deportment, to make him think I do not want him, and that will make him the readier to admit me to his friendship again, I believe, the soonest of anything but downright impudence, and thrusting myself, as others do, upon him, which yet I cannot do, nor will not endeavour." [62]

But there are freer and easier and gayer relations with men than these difficult and ceremonious dealings with peers and chancellors. There are hours of forgetful, careless jollity, when the good meat warms, and the wine flows, and office cares and domestic worries cease to trouble. Pepys's predilection for the bottle seems to have been mainly social and one would never imagine his having either time or taste for solitary drinking. But good company and good fellowship were too apt to lead him astray, and the excesses were duly regretted the next morning. Yet I do not imagine they were very serious or very hurtful, and one gets many a vision of merry outings, of joyous dinners at country inns, of hours gaily spent in song and jest and the pleasant exchange of words that were light-hearted, if not deep-thoughted. It is evident that the Diarist liked good company and could be good company himself.

Also, there was much more grave and serious intercourse, intelligent talk with intelligent men on matters that were worth while. There is Mr. Hill, with whom one can discuss music, or the universal character, or the art of memory, or Granger's counterfeiting of hands, "and other most excellent discourses to my great content, having not been in so good company a great while, and had I time I should covet the acquaintance of that Mr. Hill." [63] Time! Time! That is what fails us for these agreeable superfluities.

Fortunately in the later years there was more leisure, and we should not overlook the charming variety of Pepys's mature friendships, both as indicated by Evelyn and as suggested in the following passage of a letter from one who knew him well: "Mr. Pepys, who entertained us with that obliging kindness which engages all that he converses with into a love and respect for his person, which time, that destroys other things, does digest into a habit, and renders it so perfect that it generally lasts as long as a man's life. Of this there has been many examples; several of Mr. Pepys's friends continuing so, notwithstanding all accidents, till death; and the rest are likely to do the same." [64]

With women of his own class, good women, sensible women, Pepys also enjoyed himself thoroughly, and liked to associate with them. Whatever different relations with women we may have to trace later, this simple, innocent converse must be remembered as going far to prove that Pepys was not fundamentally vicious or corrupt. It is true that he preferred the handsome faces and registers his disgust at finding Mrs. William Montagu far from the beauty he thought: "It put me into an ill humour all the day." [65] And that deadly, frank, straight criticism withers pretence, withers conventional compliment. If the women are fools and fussed and feathered, let us — not tell them so, we are too polite for that, but let us at least set it down in those dear pages where our recompense for manners comes. "The rest of the company of the women were all of our own house, of no satisfaction or pleasure at all." [66] Yet there are many who are approved, and approved not for mere looks, but for gravity and good counsel and sober carriage. Mrs. Buckworth is commended "for her gravity above any in the parish." [67] Mrs. Clerke is not handsome, but is "a woman of the best language I ever heard." [68] And there is another lady, not named, "that hath not one good feature in her face, yet is a fine lady, of a fine taille, and very well carriaged, and mighty discreet." [69] Altogether, there are few things more delightful than to pass an afternoon in the sweet, gay, innocent company of a parcel of gentle and frolicsome girls. "Where, when we come, we were bravely entertained and spent the day most pleasantly with the young ladies, and I so merry as never more." [70]

IV

How Pepys appeared to the young ladies we shall never know. I do not imagine him quick and sprightly in conversation, inexhaustible in wit, always ready with that ingenious repartee, which sets the air asparkle, even though with a mere inflammation of nothing. He may have had these gifts, but the Diary does not suggest them, and I have an idea that, when he did not force himself into a slightly labored gaiety, he was inclined to be quiet, to watch and make internal notes, and even, in delicate situations, to be a trifle awkward. The self-consciousness, the embarrassment, which he admits on more than one occasion, must have often beset him. "Anchovies, olives, and muscatt; but I know not yet what that is, and am ashamed to ask." [71] This sort of shame is a terrible social handicap. In fact, with sensitive persons, the greatest of all social handicaps is one's self, which somehow intrudes a gigantic, blighting shadow between the eager spirit and all forgetful enjoyment, and I have no doubt that Pepys knew the monstrous shadow well, though he may not have analyzed it in that form. Something of this is what he means when he says, "it is my nature not to be forward in visits." [72]

Indeed, social as he was, it is evident that he also knew the shrinking from all society, the sense of its hollowness, its insufficiency. In the midst of the gayest and most gleeful social occasion he would have well understood the damning comment of Sly the tinker, in "The Taming of the Shrew," as the lively farce is enacting before him: "'Tis a very excellent piece of work, Madam Lady: would it were done." When the company is gayest about him, and the laughter merriest, Pepys's soul suddenly stops like a run-down watch, and with a sigh he registers: "So to supper with them at Sir W. Batten's, and do counterfeit myself well pleased, but my heart is troubled and offended at the whole company." [73] When the jests are flying thickest and each man is telling loudly large anecdotes of his own achievement, the perverse little devil at Pepys's elbow makes his diabolical comment: "a great many silly stories they tell of their sport, which pleases them mightily, and me not at all, such is the different sense of pleasure in mankind." [74]

And when you are most in the mood for jollity, when care has left you for the moment, and the heart is light and the heels lighter, you may go out with great expectations, and all your hope may be thwarted by some untoward circumstance. Pepys dines with a friend; but the appearance of the friend's aged mother is such as to damage appetite, and the presence of a sick wife does not add to the hilarity. [75] He gets a charming company to dinner, but the folly of one individual sets his sensitive nerves all a-jangle: "My simple Dr. do talk so like a fool that I am weary of him." [76] The food may be excellent and the guests may be estimable; but they are not your kind, not those to whom your spirit opens with natural cheerfulness: "We were as merry as I could be with people that I do wish well to, but know not what discourse either to give them or find from them." [77] Alas, how many such occasions we all have to live through, and this master of words has put the experience perfectly.

Also, the company may be delightful, and you may know it, a choice gathering of your nearest friends, with whom you ought to find pleasure, if with any one. Yet you may be simply out of the vein yourself, there may be some little pricking sting of office care, or you may be a few shillings wrong in your accounts, or there may have been a trying domestic scene during the day, and you are unfit for pleasure, and the gayest merry-making in the world sounds like the crackling of thorns under a pot. And you leave the others to their sporting, and turn away to bed, to forget them and yourself in sleep — if you can: "Then home and to my office late, then home to bed, leaving my wife and people up to more sports, but without any great satisfaction to myself therein." [78]

Yet, if you have the social chord in you, and Pepys undoubtedly had, as most of us have, somewhere, the contact of your fellows will pull you at times out of even the worst of these blue fits. Your nerves will begin to thrill and quiver, the corners of your mouth will lift at the tinkle of laughter. The sight of a gay company absorbed in a game will stir you, so that you long to be with them. Cards? In the abstract Pepys does not care much for cards. When he loses sixpence, it is annoying.[79] When he wins nine shillings, it is most agitating, and he prays God it may not tempt him to play again.[80] Aunt Wight endeavors to teach him gleek; but he is rather lofty about it and, the truth is "have not my head so free as to be troubled

134

with it." [81] Yet, after all, these cards are strange, diverting things: there is oblivion in them, there is triumph in them, best of all, there is laughter, a chance to laugh one's self, and to see pretty women laugh, and to sit near them, and to melt away an evening in mutual, contenting gaiety. And there are other trifling games, such as "Love my love with an A," which Pepys has even seen the dukes and duchesses play at Court,[82] silly, idle things, to be sure, yet somehow they have a singular felicity in making hearts dance and eyes sparkle. And there are far more serious sports, cock-fighting, and bull-baiting, rather hideous in themselves, but hugely interesting when you watch and enjoy the crowd.

If you want really to forget yourself and your troubles, perhaps the best of all means is to go on a journey, with a frolic cavalcade, like Chaucer's Canterbury Pilgrims. Little incidents and queer faces turn up, and set everybody quipping and jesting. You revel in the sunshine and you smile at the rain. You clatter through the mud, and you brush off the dust. What do rain or dust matter to a merry heart? And you are so exhilarated, so clean intoxicated, by the mere fun of the thing, that you play all sorts of giddy pranks which would seem strangely out of place in staid London. There is that delightful trip through

Rochester and Dartford: "Of all the journeys that ever I made this was the merriest, and I was in a strange mood for mirth. Among other things, I got my Lady to let her maid, Mrs. Anne, to ride all the way on horseback, and she rides exceeding well; and so I called her my clerk, that she went to wait upon me. . . . By and by we come to two little girls keeping cows, and I saw one of them very pretty, so I had a mind to make her ask my blessing, and telling her that I was her godfather, she asked me innocently whether I was not Ned Wooding, and I said that I was, so she kneeled down and very simply called, 'Pray, godfather, pray to God to bless me,' which made us very merry, and I gave her twopence. In several places I asked women whether they would sell me their children, but they denied me all, but said they would give me one to keep for them, if I would. Mrs. Anne and I rode under the man that hangs upon Shooter's Hill, and a filthy sight it was to see how his flesh is shrunk to his bones." [83] Yet, for all the corpses, it was a merry and diverting journey.

And there is the wild frolic at home, when they all had just a trifle of wine, to lighten their spirits, and then fell to dancing, and Pepys and W. Batelier and one M. Banister put on women's garments, and Mrs.

Pepys and Pegg Pen and Nan Wright put on periwigs, "and mighty mirth we had and Mercer danced a jig." [84] It may not have been a very wonderful jig, but Mercer was pretty and graceful, and on those sorts of occasions every thing is wonderful to enjoy and pleasant to remember, when the limbs are old and stiff and not fit for dancing any more.

Pepys's general attitude towards dancing is interesting. In the earlier days of the Diary he expresses some disapproval of it, perhaps under the influence of his Puritan training. He dislikes to see young girls exposed to the vanity of dancing school,[85] and goes away from a social dancing-party in disgust.[86] His own first attempts are made at an age when a man rarely learns to dance well, and he is astonished at himself for venturing such a thing.[87] Yet, when the habit is once formed, he seems to enjoy it amazingly, and many delightful scenes of the Diary have dancing as a conspicuous feature of them.

But unquestionably Pepys's most attractive social aspect is as a host. He did love to gather his friends about him and entertain them and feed them and be himself the wildest of the lot. The blend of ostentation and pride and agonized economy and gay abandonment and real, hearty kindliness, which appears in page after page of the Diary, as it describes these social meetings, is as fascinating as it is thoroughly human. I have already quoted, in connection with Pepys's money, one sigh of relaxed restraint, when he decides to forget scruple and enjoy himself; but I must refer to another, even more delicious: "So away to bed, weary and mightily pleased, and have the happiness to reflect upon it as I do sometimes on other things, as going to a play or the like, to be the greatest real comfort that I am to expect in the world, and that it is that that we do really labour in the hopes of; and so I do really enjoy myself, and understand that if I do not do it now I shall not hereafter, it may be, be able to pay for it, or have health to take pleasure in it, and so fill myself with vain expectation of pleasure and go without it." [88]

The climax of all Pepys's social ecstasy occurs near the end of the record, when ampler means permitted indulgence with less scruple. This magnificent orgy of hospitality would be merely dimmed by comment or expatiation: "We fell to dancing, and continued, only with intermission for a good supper, till two in the morning, the musick being Greeting and another most excellent violin, and theorbo, the best in town. . . . And so broke up with extraordinary pleasure, as being one of the days and nights of my life spent with the greatest content; and that which I can but hope to repeat again a few times in my whole life. This done, we parted, the strangers home, and I did lodge my cozen Pepys and his wife in our blue chamber. My cozen Turner, her sister, and The., in our best chamber; Bab, Betty, and Betty Turner, in our own chamber; and myself and my wife in the maid's bed, which is very good. Our maids in the coachman's bed; the coachman with the boy in his settle-bed, and Tom where he uses to lie. And so I did, to my great content, lodge at once in my house, with the greatest ease, fifteen, and eight of them strangers of quality." [89] Oh, what a regal night!

V

PEPYS AND HIS INTELLECT

I

PEPYS had a normally clear and vigorous intellect and liked to use it. He reflected upon life, the movement of the world, and the souls of men and women with more or less logical analysis, and always with curious interest.

Placed as he was, in such surroundings and circumstances, he could not fail to be impressed with the mutability of fortune. Constantly he applies his keen intelligence to the shifts and changes of men's positions: up in the world one day, down the next, now debased, now exalted, and he draws significant if not profitable conclusions, as to the wisdom of hoping little and counting on nothing. Sir George Cartaret, what a great figure he seems, securely established and unshakable, bowed down to everywhere by little petty persons. Yet he, who the other day was so great that nobody durst come nigh him, grows "as supple as a spaniel, and sends and speaks to me with great submission, and readily hears to advice." [1] Which ought to make one humble, but I don't know that it does.

It must be confessed that the result of a vast num-

ber of such observations is a certain pessimism in
the Diarist, a tendency to emphasize the darker side of
human nature. There is a bitter rule of Mr. Falconer,
to the effect that every man who proposes any project
should be suspected to be a knave, or at least to have
his own ends in it, which is, on the whole, rather approved.[2] And there is the cynical suggestion that
when a man like Sir R. Holmes, a good man too, and
one whose friendship is worth having, makes special
professions of kindness, it is just the time when one
ought to be suspicious.[3] Nor is the darker implication
much lightened when a shade of satire, something not
very usual in Pepys, insinuates itself: "Mighty merry
to see how plainly my Lord and Povy did abuse one
another about their accounts, each thinking the other
a foole, and I thinking they were not either of them,
in that point, much in the wrong." [4]

Yet it must be remembered, as regards this cyni-
cism, that the world in which Pepys chiefly moved,
though intensely human and full of quickly crossed
and twisted motives, was a very limited and peculiar
world, a world adapted to blight kindness and charity,
if ever there was one; and the really wonderful thing
is that in such an atmosphere Pepys kept so sane and
kindly and broad-minded as he undeniably did.

But, kindly or unkindly, there is no question about

his delight in the observation of human nature, or his perpetual application of his sharp wits to the study of it. Take, for example, his curious comments on Lord Fitzharding's discussion of Prince Rupert's courage, how ready and quick and self-forgetful he might be in a fight, and yet how he drooped and wavered like another man at the prospect of death by a hateful disease.[5]

It is to be noted, further, that Pepys is quite as merciless in applying intellectual scrutiny to himself as to others. A certain amount of distinction is needed here. It is impossible to regard Pepys as being a profound scientific student of his own consciousness, like Amiel. He has not the equipment for any such study, does not take things from a large enough point of view, is not enough of a trained abstract thinker. He does not relate his own motives or spiritual conditions to general principles, or only very rarely. We may best express it, perhaps, by saying that he reflects himself and his own life and actions much more than he reflects upon them. But the reflection, whatever its nature, is extraordinarily intense and vivid.

He never hesitates a moment to commend himself. Yet the commendation is so naïve, so childlike, so winning in its simplicity, that you cannot class it as offensively vain. Besides, it is apt to be justified.

How charming is his effort "to make a song in the praise of a liberall genius (as I take my own to be) to all studies and pleasures, but it not proving to my mind I did reject it and so proceeded not in it." [6]

As to fault-finding, it is unnecessary to remark how free Pepys is with it. It is not only the larger, impressive sins, which one takes a certain pride in, even while one reprehends them; it is the mean, petty, sneaking vices, which Mark Twain declares he found it utterly impossible to record in his Autobiography, however hard he tried. Pepys records them as perhaps no other human being ever did.

But what is most charming in Pepys's analysis and reflection of himself is the attitude of pleased wonder with which he surveys his own doings and experiences, as if they belonged to some other person, from whom he was completely detached. This attitude appears all through the Diary and is one of its greatest attractions; but I do not know that it is anywhere more delightful than in the account of the inspection of the tomb of Queen Katherine of Valois: "I had the upper part of her body in my hands, and I did kiss her mouth, reflecting upon it that I did kiss a Queen, and that this was my birth-day, thirty-six years old, that I did first kiss a Queen." [7]

Also, Pepys has, in no inconsiderable measure, that

greatest profit and benefit of analytical reflection, the power of putting one's self in the place of others. How often, when he has been finding fault, does he pause and consider and add that, after all, the other fellow is doing no more than he should have done in the same circumstances.

Not only had Pepys natural intellectual powers. It is evident that they were well trained, and constantly employed for specifically intellectual purposes. We have already seen that the chief definite record of his university life was a drunken frolic. But he must also have made much more serious use of his time. He learned the languages, both ancient and modern, and was familiar with what a gentleman was in those days expected to know. However he may have wasted some childish hours, like most of us, he liked to look back to those unwasted, as, for that matter, to the wasted ones also. He has many affectionate references to his schoolfellows. Moreover, he is inclined to think that the teaching and the learning were more profitable in his youth than what he sees about him later, and I have known men who were like him in this point, as in others: "Truly I find that we did spend our time and thoughts otherwise than I think boys do now, and I think as well as methinks that the best are now." [8]

Though he was never an elaborate mathematician and even speaks of learning the multiplication-table at a time when he had already been long established in the Navy-Office,[9] Pepys had always a great love for scientific matters. His intense and vivid curiosity made him alert for new observations and discoveries, both theoretical and practical. He liked astronomy, endeavored to teach Mrs. Pepys the rudiments of it, wished to be roused to see the comet,[10] was interested in the movements and manifestations of the heavenly bodies, and expressed his gratitude for all he had learned about them when the moon helped him out of a dark wood at night, "which recompences me for all the pains I ever took about studying of her motions."[11] He liked political economy, was anxious to inform himself about the working of commerce and exchange and the various complicated principles of finance.

Combining his social with his scientific tastes, he was always on the lookout for somebody who could tell him some significant or startling fact, enjoyed talking with old sailors of the wonders of the sea, or getting hold of travellers and pumping them as to the manners of strange countries. And though he reports some remarkable tales, his native common-sense and critical instinct prevented him from being grossly imposed upon.

Also, he was tempted to buy scientific instruments, and liked them well and carefully made and consequently expensive. When Reeves visits him on a mighty fine bright night, he is delighted, and, though very sleepy, goes forth upon the leads and inspects the moon with rapture through a twelve-foot glass and immediately resolves that he too must have such a glass, that he may enjoy such delights more often.[12] And the microscope appeals to him as much as the telescope.

He is as eager to learn from books as from the talk of experts, and sits up nights and strains his eyes to wade through scientific treatises, though sometimes they are too abstruse for his unaccustomed powers. Mr. Boyle's "Hydrostatics" is "a most excellent book as ever I read," and "I will take much pains to understand him through if I can."[13] The same author's book of colors is read with assiduity, "only troubled that some part of it, indeed the greatest part, I am not able to understand for want of study."[14] Also, he appreciates that both books and talk need to be supplemented by experiment and that the actual facts of nature are more stimulating to curiosity than anything that can be said or written about them. He watches with passionate interest the experiments of others, whether on animals or on inanimate objects, and he is ready himself to try anything that comes in his way. He is not only interested in fact, he wants it related to generalization, and is very impatient with Reeves, when he appears to understand "the acting part, but not one bit the theory, nor can make anybody understand it, which is a strange dullness, methinks." [15]

These scientific tendencies naturally led Pepys into the Royal Society, and he was early and long an esteemed and active member of that Institution, the activity culminating in his presidency for two years, from 1684 to 1686. The Diary mentions his original admission to the Society on the fifteenth of February, 1665, and at once registers the interest he never lost: "It is a most acceptable thing to hear their discourse, and see their experiments." [16] It is true that, with the usual candor, he confesses that he was sometimes out of his depth, "here was very fine discourses and experiments, but I do lacke philosophy enough to understand them, and so cannot remember them." [17] Yet his attendance was constant and there is no question but his general profit was great.

The best fruit of all this zeal was a more or less intimate acquaintance with most of the leading scientific men of the day. Pepys records his dealings with them with deference and becoming humility, yet their peculiarities are set down with the same bare truth that is applied to the princes and the maid-servants. Thus, there is Mr. Hooke, the geometrician, "who is the most, and promises the least, of any man in the world that ever I saw." [18] Pepys's connection with Sir Isaac Newton belongs to a later period than that of the Diary; but one would hardly wish a better tribute than to have Newton write: "How ready I should be to serve you or your friends upon any occasion." [19]

Nor was Pepys's intellectual enthusiasm confined to scientific subjects. Though perhaps not very profound or systematic, it was universal, and turned to every phase of speculative and practical thought. He liked to get a group of intelligent men together and hold rich and rambling discourse with them on the large questions of life, rambling, that is, in the charming sense, that one topic leads to another and strange and new considerations amply unfold themselves through the long hours that seem too short. For instance, there is the full, delightful conversation with Sir George Askew and Sir William Petty.[20] Or again, he was perfectly content to suck the sweet of thought from old books. Books! He had a real passion for them. Why, when he visits Sir Philip Warwick and finds him busy, he settles down in the library, picks up a volume of Erasmus, and is so enchanted with one chapter in it that he has much ado to keep from tearing out the page and stuffing it in his pocket.[21] Books! What is there in this busy, driven, fretted life of a public official to compare with them? And he sighs to be "quietly settled with what little I have got at Brampton, where I might live peaceably, and study, and pray for the good of the King and my country." [22]

II

In literature more narrowly so-called Pepys's interest is quite as great as in the more abstract aspects of thought. One has been an author one's self, or tried to be, or wished to be; and when that is the case, one is always interested in writing as a fine art. No person who has attempted authorship — and in these days who has not? — can fail to be touched by Pepys's comment when, with a sigh, he tears up the romance of his youth, by the title of "Love a Cheate": "a romance I begun ten years ago at Cambridge; and at this time reading it over to-night I liked it very well, and wondered a little at myself at my vein at that time." [23] In later years the authorship, though highly intellectual and creditable, was of a more sober order — as, alas, with so many of us — Memoirs of the

149

Navy, elaborate plans for Histories of it, and such like; but the sense of literature was there all the while. Indeed, how could it have been absent from the man who wrote that Diary? And I so often wonder how he would have relished the wide, enormous glory that has enveloped him with the passing years. In itself he would have relished it, but coming from those strange barings and strippings of the inmost soul — ? Yet I am almost sure he would have relished it anyway. An author is an author.

Pepys's interest in imaginative literature was not confined to the youthful writing of it. He frequently reads the plays that he has seen on the stage, sometimes liking them better in print than in the actual performance, sometimes not so well. His wife reads plays to him, as well as other things, and they both enjoy it. He reads novels and hopes that God will forgive him for spending a whole Sunday in the perusal of French romances.[24] On another occasion he permits himself to read a collection of French stories of an extremely vivacious character. This is a doubtful proceeding, as he recognizes; still, it is a sort of thing that it "do no wrong to read once for information sake." [25] As we find in Shakespeare, when you are learning a language, you have to learn the worst word in it, and then you forget it, of course. And

Pepys's conscience is made perfectly comfortable by destroying the book afterwards: "After I had done it I burned it, that it might not be among my books to my shame." [26]

It appears that the Diarist, again like the average man, was not any great lover of poetry. He turns to Chaucer occasionally, with a certain amusement,[27] picks up a volume of his contemporaries now and then, say Dryden, say Cowley, say Butler, reads, of course, plays in verse as well as in prose. What saves his memory in the poetical line is his devotion to the old ballads and the magnificent and most valuable collection of them which formed an important part of his much-prized library. His zeal in the pursuit of these shows charmingly in a passage of one of the letters of his last years: "If you could prompt me to any means for my coming to more knowledge of the volume of ballads you mentioned yesterday, wherein was that of the battle of Agincourt, I should gladly look after it." [28]

Pepys naturally met most of the famous literary men of his time. The greatest of all, Milton, does not appear in the Diary and is only indirectly referred to in a letter of one of Pepys's correspondents.[29] But Dryden is introduced quite frequently and at a later period Pepys seems to have known him well. The poet writes, in answer to some request, "any desire of yours is a command to me,"[30] and Pepys rejoins on the same day, expressing his obligation and urging his friend to partake of "a cold chicken and salad."[31] We get a second-hand glimpse of the grave and dignified figure of Cowley,[32] and Evelyn is always waiting round the corner for a chat. One of the most winning of these literary apparitions is that of old Thomas Fuller, whom Pepys takes to the Dog Tavern for entertainment, where Fuller regales him with feats of that extraordinary memory and intellect, among other things mentioning "that he did lately to four eminently great scholars dictate together in Latin, upon different subjects of their proposing, faster than they were able to write, till they were tired."[33]

But the mere external gossip of the Diary, picturesque as it is, is of less interest to us than the revelation of the Diarist's own view of things; and his opinions in literature have the same charm as in other matters, that of complete freshness and independence. They have a certain value in themselves, but a far greater value as portraying him. And, as always, his attitude is that of the ordinary man of the world, not particularly sensitive to the finer things of the imagination, impatient of the morbid or the subtle, prone to ask for daylight and common-sense. But the ordinary man, in such connections, is apt to keep his thoughts to himself, or, if he is forced to utterance, to say what he hears the critics say or what he thinks would please his wife — or displease her. Such is not the method of Pepys, at least not in the sacred pages of the Diary. If a classic bores him, he says so. If a popular author disgusts him, he says so. Though all the critics in the world praise, it makes no difference. He may regret his recalcitrancy; he will not conceal it. And when one is thoroughly impressed with the truth of Sterne's remark, that "of all the cants which are canted in this canting world, though the cant of hypocrites may be the worst, the cant of criticism is the most tormenting," one welcomes Pepys's frankness with delight, even when he commits the last of sins, that of differing from one's self. A lord write verses? And we must go down on our knees and admire them, because he is a lord? No, sir! "Thereabouts I to a barber's shop to have my hair cut, and there met with a copy of verses, mightily commended by some gentlemen there, of my Lord Mordaunt's. . . . But, Lord! They are but sorry things; only a Lord made them." [34] As for "Hudibras," the best seller of the day, Pepys simply cannot go it at all. He buys it and is bored and sells it again. [35] Then he buys another copy and makes another effort. [36] No use whatever: the stuff is not to his taste, and there is no more to be said about it.[37]

The same infinite freshness of attitude makes the charm of all Pepys's æsthetic experiences, of which the Diary records so many of all sorts. Take nature. It must be confessed that the man was a citizen by habit and temperament. Perhaps the Earl of Clarendon's remark to him, in his old age, as to a trip to the country, "I think you were never so long in the country before since you knew the world," was somewhat exaggerated.[38] He was familiar with the country as a boy and he often thought he sighed for country quiet; but his normal atmosphere was London, as it was Charles Lamb's; London, with its noise and its dirt and its bustle and its endless excitement. What impresses me perhaps most of all about the Journal kept at Tangier is the utter absence of any suggestion of the exotic, tropic surroundings. It is men and their doings and misdoings that interest Pepys. As for palms, and camels, and desert sands, they may go hang: "Walk by moonshine in the fields under the wall, think of our affairs: a glow-worm shining; very small compared to what we have in England." [39] That is all a tropic night meant to the administrator of the British Navy.

Yet, like so many other vigorous animal organizations, Pepys evidently felt the natural world, the influences of the sky in beauty and terror, and even subtler things in an obscure but haunting fashion. A brave morning exhilarates him. A dull, damp mist depresses him. He likes to walk in Spring Garden: it is not only "pleasant and cheap going thither," but a man may "hear the nightingale and other birds." [40] Above all, he has his own secrets for rendering what he does feel, which secrets perhaps consist chiefly in making no secret of it whatever: "Thence home, and with my father took a melancholy walk to Porthome, seeing the country-maids milking their cows there, they being there now at grass, and to see with what mirth they come all home together in pomp with their milk, and sometimes they have musique go before them." [41]

(Pepys was always greatly interested in painting. It pleased both his vanity and his artistic sense to have his portrait painted and that of his wife, and he had recourse to the best painters then available.)This necessarily involves glimpses of the painters themselves, and we have suggestive accounts of Hales, of Cooper, and especially of Lely, whose likenesses, not only of Pepys but of others, as well as his methods, are discussed with entire freedom. In the later correspondence there is a curious exchange of letters with

Kneller, showing the artist's susceptibility to criticism and Pepys's affectionate tact in appeasing it: "For God's sake, my old friend, look once more over my letter of yesterday, and tell me what one word there is in it that should occasion any syllable of what my man brings me from you this morning." [42]

As to pictures generally the criticism is as frank and stimulating as with other things; only the tone is somewhat less positive than with books, since Pepys was here more keenly aware of his limitations. Still, he usually knows his own mind. When he inspects the large collection of his cozen Turner, he frankly admits that "there are so many bad pictures, that to me make the good ones lose much of the pleasure in seeing them." [43] When he finds something that he likes — alas, a pure piece of realism, with drops of dew so natural that he feels of them again and again, to assure himself of their unreality — he is willing to pay any price for it: "a better picture I never saw in my whole life; and it is worth going twenty miles to see it." [44] He labors over his judgment, goes to the vast gallery in White Hall, finds himself utterly perplexed among so many, then is pleased to observe that he makes distinction, then leaves and returns to Mr. Hales's smaller room and thoughtfully compares what he sees there with what he has been inspecting. [45]

SAMUEL PEPYS
Portrait by Sir Godfrey Kneller

But even better than his actual criticism is his rendering of the impression made by an abundance of artistic richness, an impression which many of us have known so well when thrust suddenly into a wilderness of beauty quite beyond our wit to grasp: "Thence he carried me to the King's closett: where such variety of pictures, and other things of value and rarity, that I was properly confounded and enjoyed no pleasure in the sight of them; which is the only time in my life that ever I was so at a loss for pleasure, in the greatest plenty of objects to give it me."[46]

III

But if Pepys's pleasure in painting was somewhat remote and confused, there were two forms of art in which he felt himself thoroughly at home, and which gave him more delight than almost anything else in life, the theatre and music. All over Europe during the Renaissance period the theatre was a popular passion; but in Spain and England it not only was a source of infinite enjoyment, but afforded the amplest means for the development of the national genius. To appreciate what such public entertainment meant to the Englishman of the seventeenth century we must realize that his was a world without our vast diffusion of news and information by printing. The newspaper

keeps men at home to find out what is going on abroad:
it joins communities, but it isolates individuals. You
ride to business beside your neighbor, and he reads
and you read, and you never say a word. In Shakespeare's England knowledge was scattered by word of
mouth. This is what more than anything else has
misled the Baconians, who emphasize Shakespeare's
lack of book-learning. Men learned by contact with
the world, just such wide, inaccurate, highly colored
wisdom as is piled into Shakespeare's plays. And this
is what the theatre meant, from Shakespeare to Pepys,
an epitome of life. You went there and opened your
eyes and ears, and life flowed into them. If you were
shrewd and knew how to disentangle the true from
the false, you profited; but whether you profited or not,
you enjoyed. A great, strong, active, formidable part
of England, the part that contributed the followers of
Bradford and Winthrop in America, hated the theatre, and by so doing lost something of eternal significance from life. But multitudes of Englishmen adored
it. Hear the quaint old Burton: "The Italians, most
part, sleep away care and grief, if it unseasonably
seize upon them; Danes, Dutchmen, Polanders, and
Bohemians drink it down; our countrymen go to
plays." [47] And there are the lovely words of one of
the old dramatists themselves:

PEPYS AND HIS INTELLECT

"O God,
What an internal joy my heart has felt,
Sitting at one of these same idle plays!" [48]

During the Commonwealth the theatre was utterly
banished. And the men and women of Pepys's generation fell upon it with a hungry zeal, which was never
sated and was ready to swallow almost anything. In
the period covered by the Diary the entertainment
was mainly supplied by two companies, D'Avenant's
and Killigrew's. There were some practical innova-
tions, the introduction of more elaborate scenery, and
the substitution of women for the boys who had formerly played the female parts. Also, the original Restoration drama begins to make its way by degrees.
But untrained and inexperienced dramatists could
not supply the general demand, and therefore the rep-
ertory consisted largely of the older plays, Shakespeare, Beaumont and Fletcher, Jonson, Massinger,
etc., often more or less revamped to suit an altered
taste; and it is these on which Pepys most frequently
comments in the pages of the Diary. With his conservative disposition, it is evident that, on the whole, he
prefers the older masters.

But a play is a play, and the fascination of it, under
all circumstances, is irresistible. These puppet per-
sonages make us forget, and give us the thrill of life

in hours when all our varied efforts cannot devise it from our own dull experience. Acting? Have we not come near acting ourselves? Been cast for Arethusa in "Philaster"? an absurd idea, to be sure, that we should ever have personated a beautiful woman! [49] But the acting of others carries us away, till we neglect common duty and common care. When we can go to see "The Bondman," of Massinger, which my wife and I do "so doat on," [50] what more need there be in life?

And of course there are drawbacks, more in this theatrical pleasure than in some others, and Pepys knew them as well as any of us. There are external drawbacks: theatres are not always comfortable places, even to-day; they were less so then. There are crowds and dirt and smells; and foolish people talk and distract you. There are internal drawbacks: you may be tired or ill or worried, and find it impossible to fix your attention. And then, just because you love the theatre so, you may expect too much and the result may be a dead disappointment. See how prettily Pepys provides for this state of mind and discounts it: "the house is better and the musique better than we looked for, and the acting not much worse, because I expected as bad as could be: and I was not much mistaken, for it was so." [51] But, with all the drawbacks, the delight remains. You laugh till your sides ache, laugh till you have laughed away all the cares of the world. And then the tenderness and pathos transport you almost more than the laughter, and others' sorrows make your own insignificant.

And if you are quick and keen-eyed, there are a hundred points of diversion besides the play itself, *audience* charming as that may be. There is the audience, noisy and dirty, but infinitely amusing. And there may be pretty ladies in the box next one, and a certain amount of attention may be paid them without impropriety. Especially if one of them gets chatting and flirting with a wit, it may be so absorbing that one forgets the performance altogether: "He was mighty witty, and she also making sport with him very inoffensively, that a more pleasant rencontre I never heard. But by that means lost the pleasure of the play wholly." [52]

And there are the actors, who may obscure the merit of the drama, or make up for its demerits. *actors* Pepys pronounces at all times, with his usual definiteness, on the good and bad points of the performers. This one is commended frankly for her legs, and another for her voice, and another for her carriage; and others are criticized for misapprehension of the author or the character or for general ineptitude.

Thus, the spectator is so saturated with the story of Queen Elizabeth that he weeps over the play about her; "but the play is merely a puppet play, acted by living puppets: neither the design nor language better . . . only I was pleased to see Knipp dance among the milkmaids." [53]

For the history of English acting, as for so many other things, Pepys is invaluable. All the great actors of his day flit over his stage and are caught in their vital personality. Hart, Lacy, Betterton, all are there. For the great Betterton Pepys's admiration is unlimited. Yet he records Betterton's failures, and a translation of "The Cid," of Corneille, is such as even Betterton's genius cannot make passable. [54] And there are the women, also, that dainty, graceful, fascinating Knepp, whose attractions were at any time sufficient to upset Pepys's not too stable emotional equilibrium. And there was Nell Gwynn, who infatuated kings as well as diarists. She and Knepp are seen behind the scenes, and they are indeed pretty and gracious, but their paint, and their talk — the less said about it the better. [55] Yet the crown of a delicious evening was "specially kissing of Nell." [56]

As Pepys was familiar with the actors, so he knew the dramatists, and exhibits them. There is Howard, and Shadwell, and the great Dryden, Dryden whose ample genius could so well afford to pronounce his own comedy, "An Evening's Love," "but a fifth-rate play," [57] a judgment in which some of us will not at all agree with him. And there is D'Avenant, the significant link between the old and the new drama, an excellent poet and a clever playwright, though he prostituted his talents. And Pepys buries him, with his peculiar gift at touching of obsequies: "There to see, which I did, Sir W. Davenant's corpse carried out towards Westminster, there to be buried. Here were many coaches and six horses, and many hacknies, that made it look, methought, as if it were the buriall of a poor poet." [58]

But again we turn, in theatrical as in all æsthetic matters, to Pepys's own personal impression of the plays he saw, because we know it will be humanly direct and sincere, however limited it may sometimes seem to us. Pepys mentions a vast number of dramatic pieces, including work of all the important Elizabethans and the beginnings of the Restoration drama in his own day. His especial pets seem to have been Ben Jonson and Massinger. In other words, he turned naturally to sturdy human truth and common-sense, rather than to imaginative poetry. And in this he probably represents the average man at all times.

His comments on Shakespeare have been a terrible crux to Shakespeare's idolaters. "Twelfth Night" "is a silly play," [59] and "A Midsummer Night's Dream" "the most insipid, ridiculous play that ever I saw in my life." [60] Other pieces are noticed much more favorably; but it is evident that Pepys would have been astonished at Shakespeare's modern reputation. We must always remember that the acting and other conditions of performance enter largely into such judgments. Also, there is Sir Sidney Lee's point that Pepys was not imaginative and Shakespeare's depth and delicacy did not touch him.[61] Pepys had his own quality of high-wrought emotion, as his love for music shows. But he was not imaginative in just the Shakespearean sense, and in a way it is precisely his lack of imagination that works upon the imagination of his readers. Moreover, it is not at all certain that, if it were not for tradition and established prestige, Shakespeare's more poetical work would not affect the mass of mankind much as it affected Pepys.

But what is delightful about Pepys's opinions is not their eternal correctness, but their intense and vivid personal truth. Sometimes he is influenced by convention and the judgment of others; but he at once admits it and so becomes as unconventional as ever.

He goes to see a poor play, which is having popular success, "and going with a prejudice the play appeared better to us." [62] He goes to see another poor play, but the house "do this day cry up the play more than yesterday! and I for that reason like it better too." [63] Sometimes he is weary and fretted about other things. He recognizes that this affects his judgment. But, no matter whether it is Shakespeare, or Dryden, or a cheap divertisement, or even Ben Jonson, he says what he thinks, sometimes contradicting himself, sometimes affirming what seems manifest absurdity, but always with absolute sincerity for the moment; and in a world of everlasting parrot-criticism who will not be grateful to him?

IV

Pepys enjoyed the theatre; but he enjoyed music even more and studied it and appreciated it with much of the enthusiasm of the genuine artist. He was certainly an assiduous and probably a respectable performer himself, upon various instruments, and he loved to sing, at all suitable times and at some that seem to us a little unusual. For example, when he was being carried on the river to transact a bit of business, he fell in with a gentleman, a perfect stranger, who was using the same boat, and finding that he was a lover of music, they sang together all the way down, "an incident extraordinary to be met with." [64]

Though Pepys was largely self-taught, he had teachers and spoke his mind about them. A man is recommended to teach the theorbo; but neither his singing nor his playing is approved of, and he is sent away quicker than he came. [65] Signor Pedro, the Italian music-master, is employed for a while; but the pupil wearies of him: his presence "spoils, methinks, the ingenuity of our practice." [66] Yet it is evident that Pepys worked hard at the drudgery so indispensable to musical performance, worked at it with the zeal which only love can give. When he has an odd minute, he picks up an instrument. When a difficulty of vocalization challenges him and his instructor expresses a frank doubt as to his ability to master it, he declares himself resolved to learn, and I feel sure he did. [67] In one of the enthusiastic musical letters of his later years he speaks of "the drudgery of a long and unassisted practice," like one who knows all about it. [68]

As with every amateur who really loves his art, Pepys's performance was for himself, not for others. His delightful vanity does occasionally peep out, as when he plays the viallin and lute in his dining-room and takes "much pleasure to have the neighbours come forth into the yard to hear me." [69] But in general he liked to sing and play alone, or with those who were doing their part as much as he was, and he rarely, if ever, troubles himself to record a compliment. When he was anxious and sad and fretted and solitary, music afforded him relief. When he was gay and light-hearted, it increased his merriment. And a bit of song put an exquisite finish to a busy and profitable day.

The late seventeenth century was a period of musical experiment and progress, and all sorts of novel instruments were tried and perfected or forgotten. Pepys was everlastingly curious about all of them. He dallies more or less, either by actual practice or at least by observation, with the lute, the dulcimer, the flageolet, the theorbo, the recorder, and others. He gets an expert to try his viall, "the first maister that ever touched her yet, and she proves very well and will be, I think, an admirable instrument."[70] The recorder he is especially determined to learn, as it is, of all sounds in the world, the most pleasing to him.[71] But his sensitive ear rebels at the trumpets and kettle-drums. They are popular and much cried up. Never mind if they are: it is at best but "dull, vulgar musique."[72]

And this ardent lover of the musical art was interested, not only in practice, but in theory. The subtle and difficult acoustic elements of it fascinated him, and he would stop Mr. Hooke in the street and get him to discourse on the subject of vibrations and the number that make up the hum of a fly's wing.[73] Even he had himself a few little ideas on the abstract aspects of the case. Musical theory, it appears to him, is in a bad way. A man has to learn it as it is actually taught. But the process is troublesome and the result unsatisfactory. He believes that he can put things on a far more scientific basis, and some day he will, yes, "make a scheme and theory of musique not yet ever made in the world."[74] Alas, life is hurried, and that Navy Office is engrossing, and there are so many things one would wish to do and could do. But the very effort and design are a charm.

At least, in odd moments, one can turn a song or two of one's own. It drives away care, if it does nothing else. "After a little supper vexed, and spending a little time melancholy in making a base to the Lark's song, I to bed."[75] And there is our song of "Beauty Retire," which engages so much of our spare time, and which "without flattery I think is a very good song."[76] At any rate, it is enchanting when Knepp sings it. And there are others, notably a setting of Hamlet's "To be or not to be" soliloquy, an odd subject for a song, you think. Nevertheless, it is dug up and adequately rendered two hundred years later, and produces a certain effect.[77]

When a man's life is so haunted by the charm of melody, when he sings away care and disappointment, and even love and hate, he naturally looks and hopes for the sense of melody in those about him. Now Mrs. Pepys was wooed and married for her face, not for her voice, and the latter, at least from a technically musical point of view, involves some disillusionment. Her husband makes heroic efforts to teach her, and I have no doubt she made heroic, if perhaps spasmodic, efforts to learn. Pepys bewails his lack of patience: "Nor I, I confess, have patience enough to teach her, or hear her sing now and then a note out of tune, and am to blame that I cannot bear with that in her which is fit I should do with her as a learner, and one that I desire much could sing." [78] He keeps at it, and she keeps at it. There are even times of encouragement, when it seems possible that she may make a musician. She is likely to learn to trill, after taking huge pains, and she is pleased and proud over it.[79] On good days her critical instructor finds real pleasure in her performance. Her ear is desperately bad, to be sure; but then her fingers are deft about everything: "Pleased with my wife's playing so well upon the flageolet, and I am resolved she shall learn to play upon some instrument, for though her eare be bad, yet I see she will attain any thing to be done by her hand." [80] Alas, resolutions of this nature, where the will of another party is involved, are apt to be balked and thwarted. And Mrs. Pepys to the end remained the lady of the exquisite face, but not of the voice to match.

There were others in the house besides the mistress of it, however. Perhaps something more could be done with them. If you hire a boy, you want him to have practical qualities, but it is also a great source of satisfaction to have one who can sing any thing at first sight.[81] Then the maids, they must be quick and tidy and helpful, of course; but it hurts nothing if they are comely to look at, and if they can sing, they are indeed ideal — from the master's standpoint, at any rate. There is Ashwell, who is a little airy in her pretensions and manners, but "has very good principles of musique." [82] And later there are Barker and Mercer, both with excellent voices, and it is a most interesting experiment to compare their styles, and see how one works by ear merely, the other by practice and method.[83] To be sure, all this is a little trying to the lady of the family, who not unnaturally dislikes to see more pains taken with her servants than with her; but it cannot be helped: "it is because that the girl do take musique mighty readily, and she do not, and musique is the thing of the world that I love most, and all the pleasure almost that I can now take." [84]

Also, there was much music outside of one's own four walls, as well as inside. Pepys comments widely on what he hears, and his judgment is spoken of with great respect by modern critics well versed in such matters.[85] We learn more or less of the noted musicians, of Henry Lawes, the friend of Milton, of Locke, of Gibbons, of the elder Purcell. Pepys refers intelligently to their works and their performances. And there was that curse of the sensitive ear and the cultivated taste, the amateur who neither knows nor cares anything about the real exquisite essence of music, but has worked hard to make himself mechanically perfect and is intent upon exhibiting himself at all times and in all places. Sometimes a voice and an ear may be so bad that you get real amusement out of it. It is diverting "to make Betty Turner sing, to see what a beast she is as to singing, not knowing how to sing one note in tune; . . . worse than my wife a thousand times, so that it do a little reconcile me to her." [86] But there are other occasions when you have to be polite, to endure, and smirk, and commend, and yawn, and wish with all your soul you were somewhere else. Oh, what a comfort it is to have that Diary, where you can freely exhale your annoyance and disgust. "They had a kinswoman, they call daughter, in the house, a short, ugly, red-haired slut, that plays upon the virginalls, and sings, but after such a country manner I was weary of it, but yet could not but commend it." [37]

There is the foreign music, also, and the debate between that and the English. These Italians are clever fellows, no doubt; they do some extraordinary things. Yet, after all, we are English ourselves, and the home strain pleases us, and "a song well composed by an Englishman must be better to an Englishman than it can be to a stranger, or than if set by a stranger in foreign words." [88]

But English, or Italian, or whoever, there are evenings of pure delight, when skilled throats and fingers make incomparable melody, and one simply forgets everything. "Here I met with Mr. Woodcock of Cambridge, Mr. Hardy and another, and Mr. Woodcock beginning we had two or three fine songs, he and I, and W. Howe to the Echo, which was very pleasant, and the more because in a heaven of pleasure and in a strange country, that I never was taken up more with a sense of pleasure in my life." [89]

Church music appears perhaps somewhat less prominently in the Diary than one might expect. Pepys and his friends often play and sing the settings of the psalms. Also, he comments upon organ performances and other elements in the church service. But evidently religious music, as such, did not take a very profound hold upon his soul. And any one who relishes the contrast between different spirits and tempers must enjoy reflecting upon what Pepys would have thought of the passage in which Cowper condemns all music not employed for a religious purpose: "If it is not used with an unfeigned reference to the worship of God, and with a design to assist the soul in the performance of it, . . . it degenerates into a sensual delight and becomes a most powerful advocate for the admission of other pleasures, grosser perhaps in degree, but in their kind the same." [90] Which assuredly Pepys would have called an attitude of mind "very curious to observe."

It will justly be remarked that in this intense and rapturous enthusiasm for music, Pepys shows himself distinctly apart from, if not above, the average, typical man, with whom we have so often connected him. It was his idiosyncrasy, and a noble and redeeming one. And we all know that there are vast numbers of human beings to whom music is a mere hubbub, or whose ears are sensitive at most only to blare and clangor. Yet it is curious to appreciate what immense progress music is daily making with the mass of mankind, and in spite of the insensibility of many, it may distinctly be regarded as the characteristic art of democracy and the modern world. When one comes to reflect upon this, one sees that it is because music is the art of ignorance and because the vast increase of possible information, beyond all human capacity of acquiring or retaining it, makes the age we live in the age of ignorance preëminently. Not that skill in music may not imply a great amount of purely technical knowledge; but to enjoy music, with its pure, direct appeal to the emotions, requires far less familiarity with history, with thought, with the past movement of the world than is needed for the other arts. And one wonders how Pepys would have felt about the vast development and complication of music in the nineteenth and twentieth centuries. Would he have revelled in Wagner and Richard Strauss and those strange, perplexing Russians, or would he have detested them?

But, whatever the significance of such general considerations, (there can be no question about Pepys's enjoyment of the music of his own day and the endless delight and solace it afforded him.)He expresses this concretely on many occasions when his rapture flows out in simple, unpremeditated enthusiasm. (He expresses it more generally, declaring in advanced life

that in music "my utmost luxury still lies and is likely
to remain so," [91] as he had proclaimed earlier, in a
phrase already quoted, that "musique is the thing of
the world that I love most.")[92] But the climax of his
musical ecstasy, and indeed, perhaps, with the "epicurism of sleep" passage, the climax of his high-wrought
expression of emotion, is the account of the wind-music performed with Massinger's play of "The Virgin-
Martyr." It would be difficult to render more intensely and completely the profound disturbance
created by melody and harmony in a sensitive spirit:
"But that which did please me beyond any thing in
the whole world was the wind-musique when the angel comes down, which is so sweet that it ravished me,
and indeed, in a word, did wrap up my soul so that it
made me really sick, just as I have formerly been
when in love with my wife; that neither then, nor all
the evening going home, and at home, I was able to
think of any thing, but remained all night transported,
so as I could not believe that ever any musick hath
that real command over the soul of a man as this did
upon me: and makes me resolve to practice wind-
musique, and to make my wife do the like." [93]

VI

PEPYS AND HIS WIFE

I

THE case of Mrs.* Pepys is peculiar. In a sense we may
say that few women of the past are better known to us
than she. Her husband's intimate record shows her in
most of the aspects of her character with his usual intense veracity. We see her grave and gay, eager and
petulant, fretful and mocking, angry and loving. We
see her ill, with all the distress and disturbance that
accompany illness. We see her well and ardent, ready
for work or play with equal zest, sharing her husband's
pursuits, or questioning them, or interfering with
them. During those ten long years it seems as if we
almost lived her life.

Yet it is hardly fair that any human being should
be so entirely judged on the testimony of another, no
matter how vivid. We have not one written word of

---

* In the *Diary* Mrs. Pepys is always referred to as "my wife." We
do not even know whether her husband called her "Elizabeth" or
"Betty" or "Bess," any more than we know what she called him.
The written abbreviation, "Mrs.," is frequently used in referring to
other ladies, as "Mr." with men. So far as I can gather from the
Oxford Dictionary, the pronunciation "Mister" came into use earlier
than "Missez," and we should probably think of "Mister Pepys"
and "Mistress Pepys." But the chronology of the matter is obscure.

Mrs. Pepys's own. We have only a few spoken words recorded by others, and we all feel how reluctant we should be to have our thoughts passed on from us in such a way as that. The desire to know how this woman viewed life in general and her husband in particular is at times almost overwhelming. It has been manifested in various clever modern efforts of divination. Mrs. Pepys's diary has been written for her, and sympathetic interpreters have endeavored to reconstruct her character and point of view.[1] Nevertheless, she remains, and must always remain, to a certain extent, a mystery, and a puzzling and delightful one.

She was a child of fifteen when Pepys married her, and she was nineteen when she first appears to us in the Diary. She was not uneducated or unintelligent, *artibus, linguis cultissima*, says her engaging epitaph;[2] but her education had been erratic. Her father was a wanderer and dreamer, and she knew something of the Continent as well as of England. Of life she knew what a quick girl knows, its good and its evil; but there is no reason to believe that she was contaminated by it. She was destined to know a good deal more of it in her married experience.

It is evident that Mrs. Pepys was by nature intensely social. She had no children to keep her busy at home, and her quick, gay, and sensitive temperament would have readily absorbed any amount of social diversion abroad. As her husband's means increased and he grew more anxious to entertain his friends, she coöperated with him to the full, did her part creditably, and was not afraid of work or care to advance his social success. I think we can easily divine her as an attractive as well as capable hostess. Yet her home life seems to have been rather solitary. Her family were usually at a distance, and she could not get much comfort or companionship from them. From her husband's relatives she did not get much comfort either, and apparently felt that the less she saw of them, the better. It is noticeable that the Diary gives no suggestion of her having any close friends of her own. Probably her wandering youth had cut her off from intimate childhood associates, such as come nearer to us in after life than any friends of maturity. It may be that she had them and her husband makes no mention of them. But he mentions everything, and it is extremely improbable that he would have passed over persons sure to affect him more or less.

Pepys occasionally recognizes his wife's isolation and deplores it, though somewhat harshly implying that she would think less about it, if she had more to do. "My wife, who indeed do live very lonely, but I do perceive that it is want of work that do make her and all other people think of ways of spending their time worse." [3] He quite agrees with her that she should have companionship, and not be forced to live so much with servants, though her protest on the subject leads in the most casual, natural, human, tragic way to one of the bitterest scenes that ever took place between them. Mrs. Pepys presented a written statement of the retiredness of her life and how unpleasant it was, most of it true, as the husband's incorrigible candor confesses. But it was too true to be borne. He simply lost his temper, and tore the paper, and tore a lot of other papers with it, among them his poor loving letters from sea, and he scolded, and she scolded, and altogether the Pepys household passed a distressing and convulsive day. [4] And the complaints recurred, and the scenes recurred, and I do not know that the loneliness was ever remedied. The truth is, what the woman wanted was the touch of childish hands and the prattle of childish voices. They never came.

So she had to make up for it as best she could, with minor and inadequate diversions. She would study: why not? He was interested in all sorts of scientific subjects; why should not she be? He teaches her

179

things in astronomy, and she listens dutifully and perhaps profits, perhaps also with a certain wonder why men should care what happens in Sirius.[5] He teaches her geography, "which she takes very prettily and with great pleasure to her and me to teach her."[6] No doubt she discerned that it was a great pleasure to Sam to teach anybody anything. Also, there are lighter forms of intellectual entertainment. There is poetry, not a complete substitute for real men and women, but it helps to while away a dull hour. And there are novels, those great, strange, soporific French romances, which no woman to-day could possibly labor through, "Great Cyrus" and the rest. Madame de Sévigné found them a mine of inexhaustible delight. They were absurd, she knew, but she simply could not resist the hero's lofty speeches and his all-conquering sword. Evidently Mrs. Pepys found a good deal of the same fascination. Then there was music, which Sam so greatly loved: she would try to do something, she would, she would. And there was painting, which much better suited her deft fingers. Yes, painting was a real pleasure. Yet how quickly she would drop them all, if Sam would ask her to go to the theatre, or to go anywhere.

Of course there was also the diversion of dress. You could make exquisite garments for yourself, you could buy them, and you could wear them; though, after all, where was the use, when there was no one to see? Mrs. Pepys was quick to note the new fashions, and sometimes too eager to follow them, at least in her husband's judgment. She greatly admires Mrs. Stewart's hair when done up in puffs, though he distinctly disapproves.[7] Also, the quickness in getting out of mourning, so natural to a young and vital spirit, is most objectionable to the critical observer.[8] But in general we may infer that Mrs. Pepys's taste was excellent, and that even Mr. Pepys thought so.

There is still another refuge for lonely feminine hearts, God; but we do not know very definitely what Mrs. Pepys did as to this. Her father, though a Frenchman, was a zealous Protestant. She herself came more or less under Catholic influences in her youth. After she was married, she reassured her father as to any falling off, telling him, with an affectionate embrace, how fortunate she was to have married a man "too wise and one too religious to the Protestant religion to suffer my thoughts to bend that way any more." [9] Yet, later, in a time of great domestic emotional stress, she confided to her husband that she was a Catholic and had received the Holy Sacrament.[10] The admission proved highly agitating, as Pepys was sensitive as to his Protestantism.

He hopes, however, that she will at least conform outwardly to the Church of England and that no scandal will result.[11] What her inner experiences may have been and how far she turned to spiritual consolation when this world became a trifle cold and lonely, we shall never be informed.

Also, we should like a little more light on her feeling toward Pepys himself. Naturally the Diary does not help us here. Before he was married, the ardent lover no doubt regarded the query, did she love him, and how much, as the most important in the world. After some years of matrimony there were other queries that troubled him more, and he probably took his wife's affection for granted, unless some momentary spark of jealousy kindled a passing conflagration. I think we may take it for granted, likewise. To be sure, she understood him, knew all his little defects and weaknesses, and sometimes resented them and sometimes played upon them. He was not a difficult man to read, and she had many long hours of the day to observe, and many long hours of the night to reflect and piece together. He was vain, and she knew it. He was selfish, and she knew it. He was erratic in his spending, eager in his pleasures, crude in his self-assertion. She knew it all, better than any one. Her pity for his follies was as great as her amusement at his fantastic scruples. That business of vows, who but a child would so play with it? The world might bow down to him, his family, who owed him everything, might caress and flatter. She knew the weak as well as the strong points, and was not going to be fooled about either. Yet I gather that she loved him, and turned to him, and depended on him, loved him perhaps all the more for the defects. Such cases are not unheard of. Whether she would still have loved him, if she had read that terrible Diary, I cannot say. It would have been a test for any love. She must have heard of it; but I doubt if she ever saw the ciphered inside of it. And, if she saw it and read it, I imagine her love would have borne even that ordeal.

II

As to her husband's feeling for her, we have plenty of light, light poured and showered upon us with a dazzling and at times a painful amplitude. The ordered and systematic exposition of their relations, as exhibited pell-mell in the Diary, would make a stout volume and one of the most fertile and human truth. As to the intensity of Pepys's devotion in the pre-matrimonial period there are numerous hints. Perhaps the most vivid is that conveyed incidentally with the account of the wind-music in "The Virgin-Martyr" already quoted, "it made me really sick, just as I have formerly been when in love with my wife." [12] Alas, we need no better evidence of his susceptibility as a youth than the many fully recorded instances of his susceptibility as a man. In their early married time they seem also to have clung together with a warm and earnest affection. They were poor and busy and tired and struggling, and domestic tenderness was about their only gleam of comfort. How charming is the later reference which Pepys makes to those old days: "Talking with pleasure with my poor wife, how she used to make coal fires, and wash my foul clothes with her own hand for me, poor wretch! in our little room at my Lord Sandwich's; for which I ought forever to love and admire her, and do." [13]

On the other hand, it cannot be denied that there is a cynical touch in Pepys's comments on marriage generally, a touch perhaps more akin to the typical masculine than to the feminine attitude. I do not know where you will easily surpass the bare bitterness of his remark upon a wedding: "And strange to see what delight we married people have to see these poor fools decoyed into our condition, every man and woman gazing and smiling at them." [14] An odd illustration of this lack of conjugal sentiment is, that, as time went on, Pepys apparently got confused as to the date of his wedding. And, what is stranger still, Mrs. Pepys seems to have been equally astray.[15]

If there had been children in the household, it would so much have altered things, for the father as well as for the mother. It is one of the deplorable losses of psychology that we have not Pepys's portrayal of himself in the paternal relation; the real tenderness, the fret and annoyance and remonstrance, the exquisite affectation of superiority and authority — all would have been there, but stamped with a vigor far beyond any words of mine. As it was, the house was silent. How much did Pepys consciously regret it? Did he have a presentiment of the feeling of even so devoted a father as Tom Moore, that "the distress of anxiety about these children almost outweighs my affection?" [16] There is the mad, Aristophanic, unquotable scene of recourse to the merry matrons who gave counsel as to means for supplying the domestic deficiency.[17] But when some prospect of paternal rejoicing comes, Pepys declares frankly, "I neither believe it nor desire it." [18] And there is his curious observation, on hearing that his sister expected to become a mother: "I know not whether it did more trouble or please me, having no great care for my friends to have children, though I love other peoples." [19] All which lends a certain cruel irony to the bit in the Latin epitaph on Mrs. Pepys, "she bore no children, because she could have borne none to equal her." [20]

In discussing Pepys's relations with his wife, it is impossible to overlook or neglect the harsh, the cruel, the mean, the bitter, the contemptible. He has recorded all these elements at length in the Diary, and in the picture of the man they are absolutely essential, however we may choose to generalize or interpret them. He may have been above the average in his official energy and in his sensibility to music. Let us hope that he was below it in his fashion of treating his wife, as he was at any rate below the American husband of the twentieth century. It seems best to get these painful scenes and humiliating incidents out of the way, to dispose of the criticism and fault-finding, and then to emphasize the substratum of enduring affection and dependence that undoubtedly existed.

The friction and irritation are not confined to any one portion of the Diary, but appear and disappear irregularly from the beginning to the end. We have seen the bitter quarrel that took place over the question of Mrs. Pepys's loneliness and her desire to have some sort of a companion. This source of complaint perpetually renews itself and cannot be quite settled. But there are other sources, some serious and natural, others deplorably trifling and recognized to be so by the parties themselves. "It troubles me to see that every small thing is enough now-a-days to bring a difference between us," says the disturbed husband.[21] Sometimes he holds his tongue and appreciates that silence goes further than railing: "So being good friends again, my wife seeking it, by my being silent I overcoming her, we to bed." [22] But he is determined in any case to have his way, or, at least, to appear to have it: "Very angry we were, and I resolved all into my having my will done, without disputing, be the reason what it will: and so I will have it." [23] Which is all very well, and has an impressive sound; but these ladies have their methods of evasion as well as of persuasion. Also, they have tongues from which bitter words as well as endearments flow too easily, and the principle of silently insisting upon obedience is glib to enounce but sometimes difficult to enforce. There are fierce exchanges of harsh language, afterwards regretted, and yet so readily renewed: "being come to some angry words with my wife, . . . I calling her beggar, and she me pricklouse, which vexed me."[24] And there are worse than words, there are cuffs and savage tweakings of the nose, things utterly unbecoming a decorous official of the Navy, things doing which he would have been ashamed to be seen by his great friends, and ought to have been ashamed to be seen by God. But he did them, all the same, and then he set them down, every one, in minute detail; and many men might have done them, but the setting down is certainly unusual: "Find my wife in a dogged humour for my not dining at home, and I did give her a pull by the nose and some ill words, ... that we fell extraordinarily out, insomuch, that I going to the office to avoid further anger, she followed me in a devilish manner thither, and with much ado I got her into the garden out of hearing, to prevent shame, and so home, and by degrees I found it necessary to calm her, and did." [25] But such things must stain and scar affection, even if they do not blight it permanently.

Let us look a little more into the detail of Pepys's haunting tendency to criticize. Take his wife's intelligence. We have seen that she was quick and shrewd. Her husband was well aware of it, knew probably that her sharp eye saw to the very bottom of some of his little foibles. When unduly provoked, he notes roughly that she is never to be trusted with her liberty, "for she is a fool." [26] But he knew that she was not, and doubtless realized that in some things she was more penetrating than he. He appreciated her finer instincts. Music, to be sure, she was not born for. But she paints charmingly, and it is gratifying to see Peg

Penn's pictures and to feel that they are "so far short of my wife's, as no comparison." [27] He sympathizes with her literary tastes and often defers to them, enjoys having her read to him; yet rasped, irritable nerves will burst out in comments that are wounding and unnecessary: "At noon home, where I find my wife troubled still at my checking her last night in the coach in her long stories out of Grand Cyrus, which she would tell, though nothing to the purpose, nor in any good manner." [28] I don't blame her for being troubled, do you?

Then there is the eternal question of money. We have already seen that Pepys was critical of his wife's household expenditure and her method of keeping accounts. Sometimes the annoyance reaches the point of manifest injustice, as in the reflection that "all my troubles in this world almost should arise from my disorders in my family and the indiscretion of a wife that brings me nothing almost (besides a comely person) but trouble and discontent." [29] Mrs. Pepys's point of view, no doubt, was very different. Why he wished to marry her was his own affair; but, having married her, he was assuredly bound to see that she dressed and lived in a manner becoming his station and to provide money to that end. Mr. Wheatley asserts that Pepys was mean, because he stinted his wife,

while indulging himself.[30] Alas, a streak of that meanness is almost universal, is it not? The truth is that
Pepys, like other husbands, was erratic. There were
good days, when money came in freely, or the dinner
was well cooked, and he was in a holiday humor of giving. There were others, when it seemed as if life was
nothing but demands. And the good days and the
bad days did not always coincide with the wife's
needs.

So she had her little devices and her great rages.
Sometimes she calmly orders things and leaves the
husband to settle the bill. Sometimes she threatens
to order them, come what may, tells him "in a spite-
full manner like a vixen and with a look full of rancour
that she would go buy a new one and lace it and
make me pay for it, and then let me burn it if I would
after she had done it."[31] Which was certainly most
unseemly conduct, but there had been provocation.

Yet, on the whole, I am inclined to think that
Pepys was fairly liberal, considering his circumstances, and what is more important, I am inclined to
think that Mrs. Pepys would have said so, if grudg-
ingly. She was his wife, after all, and, independent of
considerations of affection, he had much of the feeling
of a man I knew whose wife was stranded in a strange
hotel and obliged to telegraph for funds. The funds

were sent, but the husband's first comment was, "to think that *my* wife should be left in a strange place without money!" That *my* might have come from Pepys, and from how many of us.

The observant, carping critic not only watched the money flow, he stood by and made remarks on the domestic management and the housekeeping generally. He should have remembered that the child was but fifteen when she was married and had little training and discipline, even for that age. Sometimes he did remember, and was patient. Sometimes he forgot, and was not patient at all. There were the servants, such a problem for a girl-wife, who never thought much of her dignity and cared little for it. It was harassing for a busy Clerk to come home to petty squabbles about wages, or about duties, or about respect. And of course the mistress had generally to be supported in her authority, even when she was wrong, and the maid had to be sent away, and another to be sought for, and there was no end of vexation and disturbance. Afterwards, it might be that the mistress had to be remonstrated with, and that was not always a pleasant or a comfortable task. "I said nothing to either of them, but let them talk till she was gone and left us abed, and then I told my wife my mind with great sobriety of grief, and so to sleep." [32] Sobriety of grief! And there are people who say that Pepys was not a stylist!

A house has to be kept clean, and what depresses a housewife is the dreary endlessness of the task. The same old dishes to be washed, the same old corners to be brushed, and always the same old dirt accumulating on them and in them. What wonder if she gets restive and wants to go out into the world and forget! Mrs. Pepys struggled with the dirt bravely, sometimes with constant effort persistently renewed, sometimes with spasmodic energy, which evokes sarcastic comment from her critical spouse: "She now pretends to a resolution of being hereafter very clean. How long it will hold I can guess." [33]

And there is the cooking. Here again Mrs. Pepys sticks to her work, and probably enjoys it more than the cleaning. She had served a strenuous apprenticeship before the servants came, and had learned her husband's tastes and how to cater to them. On the whole, her table, both on domestic occasions and for visitors, even of distinction, is generally approved.

In the main, also, Pepys is satisfied with his wife's appearance and bearing in social connections. Sometimes he betrays that irritation with the company-manner, which we are all so apt to feel with those whom we know and love in their more homespun fash-

GLAZED STONEWARE BUST OF MRS. PEPYS

By John Dwight of Fulham

ions, as in the instance already quoted when he reprehends the lady for producing her reminiscences of
"Great Cyrus" in a public place. Sometimes some
minor detail of dress strikes him as inappropriate, and
if he is tired or fretted, he breaks out with inexcusable
impatience. Mrs. Pepys puts on a fashionable arrangement of false hair, and is scolded with astonishing and
indecent violence: "Swearing, by God, several times,
which I pray God forgive me for, and bending my fist,
that I would not endure it. She, poor wretch, was surprized with it, and made me no answer all the way
home." [34] Yet, broadly speaking, Mrs. Pepys was
well dressed, she was gay, she was tactful, she was gracious, and the sort of wife to do a husband credit, no
matter how high a sphere he might be called upon to
move in. Pepys knew this well, and he often was
proud of her.

III

ALSO, he loved her, and the love endured and clung,
and makes itself repeatedly manifest, through the
petulance and ill-temper and unpardonable abuse.
No doubt he married her, to begin with, for her superficial personal charm. Then, in a few weeks, he dis-
covered that he had married, not an angel nor an artistic masterpiece, but a human being. The same dis-

covery has been made some billions of times since the world began, and always with the same shock and disillusionment. Afterwards those who are wise, or fortunate, recognize that it is possible to live with a human being, by making some compromises, and even to become attached by bonds of habit, association, and mutual understanding and interest, which last when personal charm is quite forgotten.

All the same, Mrs. Pepys was a picture and continued to be. To be sure, we do not find much of it in the likenesses that have come down to us. There is a heaviness and woodenness about the features, which must have been compensated by something the painter could not catch. But Pepys, an experienced connoisseur, admired her greatly, not only before marriage, but long after. Even towards the close of the Diary, when she is brought into competition with the court ladies, he is quite satisfied with the result: "My wife, by my troth, appeared, I think, as pretty as any of them; I never thought so much before." [35] This exultation is much increased by the enthusiasm of others. Pepys overhears Talbot and W. Hewer making the same remark to one another, and his conjugal pride is mightily exalted.[36] How much more is this the case, when he observes that "the King and Duke of York minded me, and smiled upon me, at the

handsome woman near me." [37] It certainly does no
harm to find that the human being you have married
is admired by the world at large as well as by yourself.
Except that it is a wicked world, especially as Pepys
lived in it, and beauty provoketh thieves sooner than
gold, and when you are the owner of an exquisite picture, you are always in dread that some one will rob
you of it, robbers being so thick about you, and you
being, alas, somewhat of a general robber yourself.

In other words, Pepys suffered the tortures of jealousy. It may be said at once that there was probably
no ground for this whatever. Mrs. Pepys had her
faults: she was a trifle extravagant, a trifle wayward, a
trifle pettish; she may have told a white, or even a
black, lie upon occasion. There is no reason to suppose that she was not loyal to her marriage vow. Her
social spirit responded to all friendly and amiable converse, she was merry and careless, and ready to accept attention and enjoy it. But she loved her husband and I do not believe she ever for a moment
thought of being untrue to him. Indeed, Pepys knew
this perfectly well, and frequently reproaches himself
with his causeless suspicion. But the suspicions would
come, much augmented by the suggestion of an un-
quiet conscience, daily intimating that, if the wife did
go astray, she was not without excuse. No doubt she

was quite aware of this state of mind, and was entirely willing to tease her distrustful lord, so far as was compatible with virtue. In consequence there are various dark shadows who hover through the pages of the Diary, perplexing and tormenting the writer of it, till he is clean at his wits' end. Above all, there is that dancing-master, Pembleton, a personable, insinuating fellow, who hangs about the house and drives the head of it almost distracted. What to do? Remonstrate? Yet remonstrance is so apt to make things worse. Keep still? I cannot. "Which do so trouble me that I know not at this very minute that I now write this almost what either I write or am doing, nor how to carry myself to my wife in it." [38] And of course it all comes out right, and is forgotten, and is again renewed, like all these spiritual torments. Yet how pretty and touching is the scene when the injured wife hands her husband a letter out of Sir Philip Sidney to read, "which she industriously and maliciously caused me to do, and the truth is my conscience told me it was most proper for me, and therefore was touched at it, but took no notice of it, but read it out most frankly, but it stucke in my stomach." [39] Alas, in that queasy stomach how many things stuck that ought to have been easily digested, or far better never to have been eaten.

196

But the affection was there, just the same, deep, tender, and enduring, though the object might have preferred a little different manifestation of it. To be sure, it sometimes took a rather patronizing form, as when Pepys, in one instance, emphasizes the great content he took in his wife's society, "she continuing with the same care and thrift and innocence, so long as I keep her from occasions of being otherwise, as ever she was in her life." [40] But there are constant proofs, all the more convincing for being casual, of the regard the two had for one another: "So home to dinner with my wife very pleasant and pleased with one another's company, and in our general enjoyment one of another, better we think than most other couples do." [41]

This underlying depth of tenderness is of course more particularly brought out in special times of stress or trial. There are the absences. Sometimes they take a journey together, as when Pepys makes the offhand remark "in ordinary fondness, 'Well! shall you and I never travel together again?'" and is taken up, and they set off for a quick, gay, charming bit of outing.[42] But there are many separations, for one cause or another, and when the lady is away the husband may divert himself somewhat unduly, but also he may sit in a corner and mope, turning to his beloved viallin for consolation: "played on my viallin a good while, and

197

without supper to bed, sad for want of my wife, whom I love with all my heart, though of late she has given me some troubled thoughts." [43]

Illness is a profound test of affection, also, and when you see the one you love in pain, stricken down by sudden and blighting torment, you forget all the little rubs and friction, and at once become aware of what love means, and what solitude means, and what great, strange queries are involved in life and death. No doubt that low, petty, intruding monster self pokes up its head even here, and when it does, we must record it. Mrs. Pepys is suffering. Pepys does what he can for her, and then goes off to bed and to sleep: "I did find that I was [more?] desirous to take my rest than to ease her, but there was nothing I could do to do her any good with." [44] Don't you know exactly how he felt? And there are other poignant, passionate occasions, when she suffers, and her suffering calls out the best and most unselfish there is in him. She is threatened with an operation and will have no one but him beside her. And he shrinks, and is glad it is averted: "I should have been troubled to have had my wife cut before my face, I could not have borne to have seen it." [45] Again, on one of their journeys, she is overcome with a strange fit of prostration, and Pepys is terrified: "I alone with her in a great chamber there, that I thought she would have died, and so in great horror, and having a great tryall of my true love and passion for her, called the mayds and mistresse of the house, and so with some strong water, and after a little vomit, she came to be pretty well again." [46]

But these intenser episodes are not needed to convince us that the two Pepys loved each other, and in spite of the ugly little outbreaks, lived on from day to day in moderate peace and content. After all, when you go out into the great world, it is restful to come home to your wife and tell her the strange things you have heard and seen. She knows the past, she knows what men and life mean to you, and a word is enough to make her understand. The world is full of restless wishes and eager hopes and bitter and blasting disappointments. It is cordial to the heart to have done with them and taste a little of the peace of home. "Up and to church, and home and dined with my wife and Deb. alone, but merry and in good humour, which is, when all is done, the greatest felicity of all." [47] As Charles Lamb so quaintly summed up the philosophy of life: "Contented with little, yet wishing for more."

And then, though in fretted moments, one may abuse one's wife's intelligence, she is a clever woman, all the same, and quick, and practical, and keen-sighted. She sees a thousand things that you do not, and can often give both comfort and advice that you are grateful for. When Pepys's mother dies, and he is feeling peculiarly desolate, he finds it soothing to turn to his wife. When he is in difficulties with his patron, Lord Sandwich, and hardly knows how to handle himself, he goes straight to his wife, tells her the whole situation, and she gives him the best of advice. She too has her social ambitions, and does not propose to be looked down upon by any one. Stand up to the lords, she says, it is a high demeanor does it. And Pepys takes her advice and profits.[48] When the office pesters and he sees no end to the perplexities, he resorts to the secure, domestic source of consolation, and finds it: "With these thoughts I lay troubling myself till six o'clock, restless, and at last getting my wife to talk to me to comfort me, which she at last did, and made me resolve to quit my hands of this Office, and endure the trouble of it no longer than till I can clear myself of it."[49] So these wives are of a certain solace and usefulness, after all.

IV

UNQUESTIONABLY what did most to wreck the tranquillity of the Pepys domestic establishment was the husband's extreme sensitiveness to feminine charm.

Other establishments have suffered upheaval from the same cause, and perhaps Pepys was not quite so singular in his sensitiveness as he imagined. He is often represented as a most debauched and vicious general lover, and certainly the promiscuity of his amours is somewhat astonishing and very reprehensible. At the same time, we must remember the extreme licentiousness of all the world about him, which explains, if it does not excuse. We must remember, also, the extraordinary candor with which he reveals what most men cover up. And as regards any general spiritual corruption, we must take into account his good repute in the world at large, his evident enjoyment of the society of pure women, which one does not look for with an essentially vicious temperament, and finally the vast amount of work he accomplished, something by no means compatible with a completely dissipated life.

But he liked to look at pretty ladies, whoever, whenever, and wherever, liked to look at them, and chat with them, and flirt with them, and make love to them. Their mere beauty, pretty lines, pretty color, pretty gestures, appealed to him, fascinated him, carried him quite off his feet. The dainty phrase of the old poet has it,

"O pitiful young man, struck blind with beauty!"

And Pepys puts the same thing in his terse, vivid prose, when he squanders money upon Doll, the pretty 'Change woman: "She is so pretty, that, God forgive me! I could not think it too much — which is a strange slavery that I stand in to beauty, that I value nothing near it." [50] He admires the ladies of the Court from a distance, he admires the housemaid near by, he admires in church and in the theatre. With spirits of his stamp a charming face carries it at any time.

What is attractive about Pepys's varied amours is the utter absence of vanity in the man himself. We have no idea whether he was fascinating to women in appearance or manner, whether he was a lady-killer, so that young and old, plain and pretty, were eager to respond to his advances. In his account of the matter he is busy only with his own experience, his own point of view, never even suggests the attitude of adoration in the object of his addresses. And this complete freedom from coxcombry is most refreshing after the professed Don Juanism, the delight in conquest for itself, that weary one in a man like Casanova, and even to some extent in Aaron Burr, whose Diary has so many points of resemblance to that of Pepys.

Yet Pepys did run after women, there is no concealing it or denying it. The Diary reeks with love-affairs, innumerable, indiscriminate, and infinitely disreputable. They naturally increase in abandon, as the years go on. At first there is restraint, doubt, a question as to how much can be attempted or accomplished. But such little hesitancies vanish in a wholesale career of unvarnished dissipation. It is not necessary to enter into the details of these affairs, but their general tone of utter immorality must be recognized and appreciated.

There are the affairs outside the domestic circle. Married or unmarried, high or low, gay or serious, ostensibly virtuous or not so, pretty faces all have their charm, and Pepys makes up to them with entire license. There are the Lanes and the Turners and the Bagwells, there are nameless adventures on any street-corner, exactly as we run across them in the Diary of Burr. And what is extraordinary is, not that Pepys should have the escapades, but that he should return home to that Diary and set them down in minute detail and with a cynical — or naïve — veracity that is too much for even the broad editorial conscience of Mr. Wheatley, who, to be sure, usually resorts to asterisks, which say more to the imagination that even Pepys could. The most curious feature of this scandalous record is the recourse to foreign languages. What is the strange, nervous inhibition which makes it so difficult for us to put plain words even to things we daily do, so hard to write them, so almost impossible to utter them? Whatever it is, it is most amusing to see how Pepys suffers from it. Plain English? Good, substantial Anglo-Saxon? No, no, fie, no! A bit of French, a bit of Italian, a bit of Latin, or Spanish, or even Greek at need, [51] jumbled as to forms in our shame-facedness, will convey the meaning decently. By all means, let us resort to it. What an unbelievable farrago of polyglot modesty is the following, to say what might have gone in English with quite as much decorum! "I would also remember to my shame how I was pleased yesterday to find the righteous maid of Magister Griffin sweeping of nostra office, elle eon the Roman nariz and bonne body which I did heretofore like, and do still refresh me to think que elle is come to us, that I may voir her aliquando." [52] If that is not a psychological curiosity, I should like to know what is. And the odd thing is that in Burr we have precisely the same, the same chaste resort to the disguise of foreign gibberish, and the same utter disregard of correctness in the use of it. "Walked out 5. Swindled out of another dollar pour rien absolument: with 2 avants [aventurières]; 1, 15 yrs; l'aut. 22; 1 ½ d. Bur och watten pr din. [bread and water for dinner]." [53] Strange ties linking humanity, in its vices as in its virtues!

But Pepys had distractions within doors as well as without, and the former, though naturally less numerous, were quite as enthralling, and far more unfortunate. Those genteel companions who were secured to relieve Mrs. Pepys's loneliness, Pepys saw to it that they were good-looking and that they were adept at music. Hence much, much domestic woe. There were the Ashwells and the Mercers and the Janes and a whole long string of them. There were sighs and hand-pressings and kissing in corners and — well, the Diary tells it all, without any mercy whatever. And finally came Deb. Willet, and she was enough, apparently, to bring destruction upon a firmer household peace than that of the Pepys family.

No doubt Mrs. Pepys's jealousy had been aroused quite properly, long before. She would have been very, very different from what she was, and very far from human, if she had submitted tamely to all her husband's amorous whims; for, though he took what pains he could to cover up, there must have been ample indications for a sensitive, watchful, often desolate wife. How pitiful and how humiliating is Pepys's agitation when his wife comes and goes in the midst of one of his adventures: "But Lord! in what a trouble was I, when she was gone, to recollect whether this was not the second time of her coming, but at last concluding that she had not been here before, I did bless myself in my good fortune in getting home before her, and do verily believe she had loitered by the way, which was my great good fortune, and so I in a-doors and there find all well." [54] But in heaven's name, what possessed the man to set these things down?

And then there comes Deb., and tragedy is let loose, and the passages in which Pepys depicts it are some of the most direct, intense, and poignant in the history of human nature. What bare, naked scenes of fundamental, primitive emotion! Mrs. Pepys at last understands her advantage. She has seen all the depths of her husband's spiritual disorder. She instinctively grasps the strange medley in his soul of affection for her, of rooted and inextinguishable conscience, perhaps above all of masculine hatred of a domestic row and feminine tears. She plays upon these chords with a skill that she never expended upon the flageolet. And Pepys knows perfectly that she is playing, yet he is quite unable to resist her. "Home to supper and to bed, where, after lying a little while, my wife starts up, and with expressions of affright and madness, as one frantick, would rise, and I

206

would not let her, but burst out in tears myself, and so continued almost half the night, the moon shining so that it was light, and after much sorrow and reproaches and little ravings (though I am apt to think they were counterfeit from her), and my promise again to discharge the girle myself, all was quiet again, and so to sleep." [55] Can you beat that? In its kind can Shakespeare? And the great, calm, ironical, passionless moon shining down upon it all! The moon, *qui en a vu bien d'autres*, as Pepys might have expressed it, linguistically.

So Deb. is discharged. But the lady is still suspicious, and she has some reason to be; for Pepys is simply infatuated. He cannot get the girl's witchery out of his head. He regrets and repents and promises and prays. But still, when her skirt switches ahead of him round a corner, or he thinks it does, his nerves are all of a-quiver, and wives and oaths and prayers are quite forgotten. Things get to such a pass that Mrs. Pepys insists on having Will Hewer go out with her husband to keep watch of him, and the husband submits, yes, tamely submits even to this. [56] But in the end things seem to be adjusted, and adjusted to the complete and entire triumph of the wife. Deb. is banished, and Pepys himself hopes that he is free of her. In one tremendous passage of utter surrender he gives himself over to the real sovereign and conqueror of his way-ward, tremulous, unreliable heart: "being most absolutely resolved, if ever I can master this bout, never to give her occasion while I live of more trouble of this or any other kind, there being no curse in the world so great as this of the differences between myself and her, and therefore I do, by the grace of God, promise never to offend her more, and did this night begin to pray to God upon my knees alone in my chamber, which God knows I cannot yet do heartily; but I hope God will give me the grace more and more every day to fear Him, and to be true to my poor wife." [57] And the phantom of Deb. does peep out once or twice, even after this; but the pathetic conclusion of the Diary announces, as if finally, "my amours to Deb. are past."

As to Pepys and his wife, there is little further to say. Her victory in the matter of Deb. leaves her in a delightfully favorable position, but we see no more of her. We know that she and her husband took that brief, charming journey on the Continent, after the Diary was abandoned, and then she dies. Sir Frederick Bridge charitably assumes that Pepys led a moral and virtuous life after his wife's death. [58] As we have no information to the contrary, perhaps this is the more humane view to take. But —. At any rate, he had to put up with housekeepers in his domestic establishment, and his energetic pronouncement as to the temper of one of them suggests that the former mistress of the household may have been often regretted: "she hath a height of spirit, captiousness of humor, and bitterness and noise of tongue, that, of all womankind I have hitherto had to do withal, do render her conversation and comportment, as a servant, most insupportable." [59] Surely Mrs. Pepys was not like this.

But we know nothing of his regret for her, except one or two formal references in letters, and we much deplore our ignorance; for of all his analyses of death and the experiences connected with it, surely none could have been more profound and fascinating than his comments on the death of his wife. We have them not. She simply goes away into darkness with the last pages of the Diary, and we see her go with a touch of infinite tenderness. Good-bye, good-bye, charming Mrs. Pepys! Having known you for ten years so intimately, we only wish we might have known you better.

VII

PEPYS AND GOD

I

WHAT religious training Pepys received from his mother, what childish prayers he murmured at her knee, we shall never know. We have already seen that the Diary does not indicate any very great respect for her character or her admonitions; but doubtless in this matter the child was different from the man. The only direct reference to the religious aspect of the relation that I have noted is argumentative: "After supper she and I talked very high about religion, I in defence of the religion I was born in." [1]

Though during the Diary period Pepys was a loyal member of the Church of England, it seems likely that in his youth his sympathies were distinctly with the prevailing Puritanism in some form, he not being the sort of man to court martyrdom for any faith, religious or political. Late in 1660 his pleasure in meeting an old schoolfellow was much tempered by the fear that his anti-royalist proclivities would be remembered,[2] and probably his anti-clericalism was not less ardent. He is apt to speak of the Puritans with respect, not to say, awe. Towards the very end of the Diary he openly admits his disposition to be civil to them, "in expectation that those fellows may grow great again," [3] and he puts his feeling on a little higher plane in the notable passage in which he criticises Jonson's "Bartholomew Fair," a play which he otherwise greatly admired: "only the business of abusing the Puritans begins to grow stale, and of no use, they being the people that, at last, will be found the wisest." [4]

Also, it is everywhere evident that the Puritan tradition had got hold of him somehow, and haunts him and hangs about him, even in his wildest vagaries. Profanity is apt to give him the shivers. He hates to break the Sabbath, hates to have others break it. And the strain of Philistinism, conventional regard for the outside, for appearances, so oddly and strongly interwoven in his nature, is always cropping up in unexpected ways. Note the queer mixture of hypocrite and Puritans suggested in his comment on some misdoing of Creed and its discovery: "This being publickly known, do a little make me hate him." [5]

If the early influence of his surroundings pulled Pepys toward the Puritans, that of his wife later might have tended toward the Catholic Church, unless it worked the other way, as is not unfrequently the case. He has some interesting contacts with Catholicism. There is the delightful visit to a monastery, in which all the little, petty, striking details are chronicled with the usual unforgettable vividness: the priest in his cell, with his hair-cloth, and his scanty garments, and his little bed without sheets, "but yet, I thought, soft enough"; [6] his cord about his waist; "but in so good company, living with ease, I thought it a very good life." [7] And the conclusion is cheerful and even suggests a moderate sympathy: "I do not think they fared very hard. Their windows all looking into a fine garden and the Park; and mighty pretty rooms all. I wished myself one of the Capuchins." [8] Somehow I cannot imagine Pepys as a Capuchin. Yet he might have made a good one.

Then there is the Catholic service. Pepys always finds the music attractive, as is natural. But the democracy puzzles and amuses him: footmen, beggars, fine ladies, zealous poor papists, and a few Protestants, come to see the show, really "I was afeard of my pocket being picked very much." [9] Otherwise he gets an impression of trickery and frivolity and pretence, beads turned over and prayers said, without any very deep impression of piety. But things are made handsome and comfortable; "and I see the papists have the wit, most of them, to bring cushions to kneel on, which I wanted, and was mightily troubled to kneel." [10] Surely this is enough to prejudice any man against the Catholic Church.

But when it got to be a question of politics, it was a much more serious matter. With his deceased wife a Catholic, and his Navy chief a Catholic, Pepys's enemies had plenty of handles for mixing him up with the prevailing excitement at the time of the Popish Plot, in 1679, and a brief confinement in the Tower was a superb antidote to any Roman leniency that may have found a lodging. In his letters of that period Pepys insists, with the most reiterated fervor on his thorough-going Protestantism, and one has no difficulty whatever in believing him.

All through the Diary, at any rate, and probably all his life, Pepys was a faithful church-goer. Though nominally an attendant at his parish-church of Saint Olave's, his church-going was quite widely distributed, and he appears now at one service, now at another, as convenience, or some notable occasion of preaching, guides or attracts him. He is often interested and full of curious, entertaining comment, of all sorts. I do not know that there is any evidence of his being profoundly touched or moved. If this happened, it must have been very rarely. That the observance was largely perfunctory, a matter of habit and early discipline, is clear from the whole tone in which he treats it. Indeed, he was much too inclined to fall asleep, and confesses it on a number of occasions, with quite brazen equanimity. Also, the sacred edifice does not always inspire him with the respect it ought, and in at least one instance he makes fun of the inscriptions on the tombs, "at which Captain Pett and I had good laughter." [11]

And, do your best to be solemn and reverent, there are always the distractions of all sorts. You may go to church with your mind full of cares and the service may prove altogether insufficient to rid you of them. Say you are jealous of that quick, vivacious, pretty lady who bears your name. When she is mixed up with that horrid dancing-master, you may keep away from church altogether, because it represents quite other things than religion.[12] Then there are those queer organs, the eyes, and the strange, misleading pleasure of them, so apt to be incompatible with devotion, or even with decorous attention. People may be looking at you, or you think they are, as in that inimitable episode of the periwig: "I found that my coming in a perriwigg did not prove so strange to the world, as I was afeard it would, for I thought that all the church would presently have cast their eyes all upon me, but I found no such thing." [13] And you are constantly looking at other people. For there are shoals

of them about you, and their clothes and their manners and the odd composure of their faces and their
behavior toward each other offer such an entrancing
feast for vision that the mind can hardly fix itself
upon the religious ceremony at all. If one is to turn
to heaven, perhaps it would be better to join the Capuchins.

There are the pious people, or those who appear so.
We regard them with respect, and a trifle of wonder.
To be sure, they are apt to be somewhat elderly ladies, and, the diversions of this world having palled,
devotion may be more natural. And yet — and yet —
can it be quite genuine? "The three sisters of the
Thornbury's, very fine, and the most zealous people
that ever I saw in my life, even to admiration, if it
were true zeal." [14] Of course, after the great fire, piety
was to be expected. A visitation of God like that
makes everybody think of Him and of other possible
fires even more dangerous and disagreeable. Church,
under such circumstances, becomes not only an obligation, but a relief: "I to church, where our parson,
made a melancholy but good sermon; and many and
most in the church cried, specially the women." [15]

But the pious people, though edifying, somehow do
not hold the attention, which naturally strays to more
agreeable objects. The young, eager faces, gleaming

215

and sparkling with the joy and light of this world, are so much more attractive. "And there heard a silly sermon, but sat where we saw one of the prettiest little boys with the prettiest mouth that ever I saw in my life." [16] And such queer things happen in church, too, things quite shattering to gravity, if your eyes are wide-awake and watchful for them. What would you think to see a new-married couple sitting in a pew hung with mourning for the mother of the bride? [17] Odd lack of tact, wasn't it? And when your mind was all set for solemnity, to see the minister pull off his surplice as if it had been a nightshirt, before all the congregation, and then go up into the pulpit to preach, might destroy all the flavor of his sermon. [18]

But incontestably the charm of church is the ladies, and if you want us to edify, they should be entirely kept out of it. No doubt heaven swarms with delicate angels, and no doubt we shall enjoy their society, if we ever get there. Meantime, there are these exquisite creatures on earth, right here, and really it is impossible to keep one's eyes and thoughts off them. Sometimes it is a mere matter of æsthetic contemplation. For example, there is the fair Butler, "who indeed is a most perfect beauty still and one I do very much admire myself for my choice of her for a beauty, she having the best lower part of her face that ever I saw all days of my life." [19] Sometimes, regrettable to relate, these dainty faces are so engaging, so provoking, that one loses one's head entirely, and leaves church and heaven and all to follow them. There is that lady who lives in a house near Tower Hill. Pepys simply "dogs" her home, and thinks her one of the prettiest women he ever saw.[20] Then there is the gay, piquant adventure of the coy maiden and the pins: "Stood by a pretty, modest maid, whom I did labour to take by the hand and the body; but she would not, but got further and further from me; and, at last, I could perceive her to take pins out of her pocket to prick me if I should touch her again — which seeing I did forbear, and was glad I did spy her design." [21] And meantime, the preacher? Ah, we had forgotten all about him.

II

STILL, the preachers too were immensely curious and entertaining as well as profitable. Some were prominent celebrities, notable divines and theologians. Pepys went out of his way to hear them, sometimes a long distance out of it, and then commented on all their peculiarities with his usual startling, delightful freedom. Dr. Fuller was most learned and in conversation most delightful, as a commentator on the Wor-

thies of England most inspiring; but he preached but
a poor dry sermon, and "I am afeard my former high
esteem of his preaching was more out of opinion than
judgment."[22] On the other hand, the famous young
Stillingfleet does an admirable piece of work, and is
heartily commended.[23] And there are bishops. One
of them preaches before the King; but the discourse
is full of abject flattery and Pepys does not like it and
says so.[24] Again, there is the bishop who arrives while
worship is going on and is expected to take part in it.
As he is "rigging himself," in Pepys's phrase, he tells
his man to find out where they are in the service. The
man listens, and hears, but cannot place it for the life
of him, and no more can the bishop. As Pepys expressed it to friends afterwards, "the man said that
they were about something of saving their souls, but
could not tell whereabouts in the prayers that was."[25]
And the bishop was much amused, and so was Pepys;
but I do not know that it was particularly edifying.
And there is the quarrel between the Bishop and the
Dean of Coventry and Lichfield, which is not particularly edifying either; but it is human, and Pepys nar-
rates it with gusto.[26]

There were minor preachers, too, men with neither
great names nor great stations, and long ago buried
and forgotten. But Pepys is just as keenly interested

in them, and portrays them perhaps with even more vivacious touches, so that the reader is as interested in them as he is. Respect for the cloth? Oh, yes, he feels it; but may it not be overdone just a little? For instance, "a learned man used to say, that if a minister of the word and an angell should meet him together, he would salute the minister first; which methought was a little too high." [27] Well, perhaps it was. And, after all, these ministers are queer. Or rather, they are not queer, but exactly like everybody else. Only it is queer they should be.

Some are square, plain hypocrites. There is Mr. Messum, who preaches such an eloquent sermon about the duty of giving a good example, "which I fear he himself was most guilty of not doing." [28] There is Dr. Jacomb, who is an adept at getting the ladies to supply him with dainties, and confesses with cunning gravity that he heard more of the Common Prayer while he was waiting in the vestry than he had done for twenty years. [29] Others again are good enough, estimable and useful in their way, but so deplorably heavy. Might they not have been even more useful in some other, plainer walk of life? There is our own rector, Mr. Mills, who, to be sure, spoke well of Pepys in later days, and Pepys thought well enough of him. Still he did make "an unnecessary sermon upon Original Sin, neither understood by himself nor the people." [30] Yet it must not be supposed that Pepys decried the profession entirely. There were plenty of honest, earnest, high-minded men in it, and he recognizes this at all times. Even a somewhat dull man might be stirred into good preaching, like Meriton, who "hath a strange knack of a grave, serious delivery, which is very agreeable." [31] And there were many others, like Dr. Crew, who could make "a very pretty, neat, sober, honest sermon; and delivered it very readily, decently, and gravely, beyond his years." [32]

Pepys was attentive to the substance of the sermons, also, much more than one might look for, when there were apt to be so many pretty faces about him. To be sure, with the sermons, as with the plays, there was the too high expectation and the consequent disappointment. Great things had been told of Mr. Alsopp, and Pepys went to hear him very eagerly, a good man, no doubt, and evidently a clever man, "but as all things else, did not come up to my expectations." [33] Which is the quaint, deceiving way life has when you let your imagination work upon it. And many, many sermons were dull. Oh, how many dull sermons there have been since the beginning of the world! And many were silly, pointless, and pre-

Styles," and c
sign of the bc
Independent

It may be s
a traditional
ology, as in p
had gone: it w
rarely indulg
general govei
accept the w
even good e
mocks occasi
out that Jui
feast: "The
the fast for
and so they
He criticizes
ment with tl
zealous to ii
the poor;[44] c
ing of church
regard to tl
was one vei
Lord Sandw
discourse, pa
perceive wh

tentious, made much more to show the ingenuity and scholarship of the preacher than to feed the hungry flock. But there were also others that were weighty and solemn and profitable and edifying, and Pepys recognizes it heartily and rejoices in them and even occasionally appears to derive some benefit. There is Mr. Floyd, who "made a most excellent good sermon, of our duty to imitate the lives and practice of Christ and the saints departed."[34] There is Mr. Fullword, of the almost unbelievably felicitous cognomen, who preached "a very good and seraphic kind of sermon, too good for an ordinary congregation."[35] And there is Mr. Gifford, whose discourse especially received the Navy official's exquisitely Philistine approval: "a very excellent and persuasive, good and moral sermon. Shewed like a wise man, that righteousness is a surer moral way of being rich, than sin and villainy."[36]

But with sermons, as with plays and poems and music, what counts is not any abstract value of Pepys's opinion, but the charming and vivid freshness of it, the absolute sincerity with which it is set down, whether favorable or unfavorable, without regard to position or reputation or distinction or prestige. One of Mr. Mills's sermons is "pungent."[37] What Pepys says is pungent always, even when one disagrees with it most entirely. With what force and

221

ration supplemented a little later by the even bolder comment, "so I see that religion, be it what it will, is but a humour, and so the esteem of it passeth as other things do." [47]

But this was at the very beginning of the Diary, and hardly expresses a permanent state of mind. An established religion was a good thing, a desirable thing, a necessary thing, possibly for the other world, certainly for this. There are a lot of points that you might argue about forever; but it is far better to take for granted what your fathers handed down to you: "There is room to cavill, if a man would use no faith to the tradition of the Church in which he is born, which I think to be as good an argument as most is brought for many things, and it may be for that among others." [48] A large portion of humanity gets along with it, at any rate.

III

As to the more emotional aspects of the spiritual life, Pepys is perhaps no more enlightening than as to the intellectual; but he is equally alive, always alert and inquiring and ready to receive facts and investigate them and give an opinion — or withhold it. The cruder and more fantastic forms of popular superstition do not appeal to him much, except as matter of scientific curiosity. He reads Glanville's book on Witches, and finds it well writ, but not very convincing.[49] He discusses some of the extensive crop of prophetic anticipations of the great fire, together with the usual dismal foretellings of greater disasters to follow, and concludes the evening by laughing at the prophecies of Lilly the astrologer.[50] In his later years he makes rather extensive inquiry into the question of second sight, amasses a considerable amount of testimony and sifts it with shrewdness, even his favorable conclusion being based on the acute remark that those who claimed to possess second sight were far from being benefited by it.[51]

As to omens and auguries and special interpositions of Providence, he proclaims a decided scepticism, though I have some doubt whether the attitude always held. To suppose that good weather came merely to suit the king's coronation and then at once gave way to thunder and lightning strikes him as too preposterous for notice.[52] In ghosts and apparitions he was fearfully interested. The appearance of the devil in Wiltshire, promenading the streets and beating a drum excites his curiosity amazingly; yet his musical instinct protests against a devil who could not pick up a tune.[53] Long years after he spends eager hours on his trip to Tangier discussing the ques-

your resolutions? Was this a common custom in the seventeenth century? I somehow cannot quite imagine Shakespeare binding himself in such a fashion, or that gay, gilded, laughing John Fletcher, or the quaint, severe, austere, superbly human old poet, Donne. Yet it would not surprise me a bit if a lot of men had done it and were doing it now. The world, the flesh, and the devil are such desperate nuisances, and if a vow or anything else will help to get rid of them, why not try it? Yes, I imagine some of your neighbors make such vows, if you do not, and read them over and recur to them as Pepys did, and get some good of them too. Only, I doubt if many women do it. That seems to me rather a man's resort than a woman's. A woman sins and stops more by natural instinct than does the fantastic imagination of a man, and a woman would see through the sham of such a thing more quickly and laugh at it. In any case, those who favor the practice would naturally not advertise it, and that is why I cried out with delight when I ran across just such a vow as Pepys's, made by a man of an entirely different type, a shrewd, sceptical, cynical self-analyst, Benjamin Constant. Does not the following, written in English by Constant in 1788, throw a priceless light on the whole business of Pepys's solemn obligations? "By all that is deemed honorable and sacred, by the value I set upon the esteem of my acquaintance, by the gratitude I owe to my father, by the advantages of birth, fortune, and education, which distinguish a gentleman from a rogue, a gambler, and a blackguard, by the rights I have to the friendship of *Isabella* and the share I have in it, I hereby pledge myself, never to play at any chance game, nor at any game, unless forced by a lady, from this present date to the 1st of jany, 1793: which promise if I break, I confess myself a rascal, a liar, and a villain, and will tamely submit to be called so by every man that meets me." [61] Note the delicious "unless forced to it by a lady." Is not that perfect Pepys?

Unfortunately Pepys gives us no such elaborate sample of a vow, written out in full detail. If he had appreciated our keen interest, no doubt he would have done so. As it is, the vows were for himself, not for us. But he refers to them at all periods of the Diary, meditates upon them, alters them, renews them, with all depth of sincerity and all solemnity of conviction. "Home and at my office till 12 at night making my solemn vowes for the next year, which I trust in the Lord I shall keep, but I fear I have a little too severely bound myself in some things and in too many, for I fear I may forget some." [62] That is mak-

charming regret of the High-Priest Calchas, in "La Belle Hélène": "*si j'avais suivi ma vocation, j'aurais été homme de plaisir.*"

The prettiest point of all in the keeping of Pepys's vows is the tricks he plays with himself, tricks such as you and I have played since we were five years old. You bind yourself in the closest possible manner, and then you immediately begin to seek loop-holes and evasions by which you can get out of it. This is a broken day, anyway, says Pepys: vows don't count, and you can do what you please.[67] Wine? Oh, no wine; but burnt wine is different, burnt wine is not included, I can drink burnt wine: "but it is an evasion which will not serve me now hot weather is coming, that I cannot pretend as indeed I really have done, that I drank it for cold, but I will leave it off, and it is but seldom, as when I am in women's company." [68] You remember Benjamin Constant might play when he was forced by a lady.

Also, there are those delightful compromises. Only so many times at the theatre? But Mrs. Pepys has an allowance also, and she has not used all hers: what if we were to beg one of her? And she agrees, of course; "so my vowe is not broke at all, it costing me no more money than it would have done upon her, had she gone both her times that were due to her." [69] Can't you imagine the scene? Pepys invoking his ingenious casuistry, and Mrs. Pepys, perfectly indifferent to his arguments and his scruples both, smiling a little queer, contented smile at the devious mental processes of her beloved lord?

But sometimes the vows are broken, straight and square, with no evasion or compromise whatever. Some unseen play lures too facile footsteps, some un-kissed mouth whispers momentary oblivion. And those solemn obligations are blown to all the winds of heaven. And repentance comes afterwards, and a dark, dreary hour: why did I do it, why, why? "Having made a vow to myself to drink no wine this week, and this day breaking of it against my will, I am much troubled for it, but I hope God will forgive me." [70] Again, "so against my judgment and conscience (which God forgive, for my very heart knows that I offend God in breaking my vows herein) to the Opera." [71] Did it pay, Pepys, did it pay? Beside the High-Priest Calchas there is that old Greek Epictetus, whom we read occasionally,[72] with his preachings about the things that are in our power and the things that are not. But our power is so deplorably unavailing against these lusts and longings of the flesh!

The only resource is to make more vows and more,

stopped, and home to cards awhile, and had opportunity para baiser Mercer several times, and so to bed." [74] Or again, how ravishingly human is the mixture in the story of the visit of Mrs. Pen's pretty maid. "So I carried her some paper and kissed her, leading her by the hand to the garden door and there let her go. But, Lord! to see how much I was put out of order by this surprisal, and how much I could have subjected my mind to have treated and been found with this wench, and how afterwards I was troubled to think what if she should tell this and whether I had spoke or done any thing that might be unfit for her to tell. But I think there was nothing more passed than just what I here write." [75] So Sisyphus goes on rolling.

IV

THERE are persons who, when they are overwhelmed by these conflicts and struggles, seek divine aid to help them out. What use did Pepys make of prayer, and what did he think of it? When his aged aunt, as is the fashion of aged aunts, points out to him the efficacy of the prayers solicited for him at the time of his operation for the stone, he agrees, but rather casually: "which I also in complaisance did own; but, God forgive me, my mind was otherwise." [76] The proper external forms of prayer are duly observed.

IVORY MEDALLION OF SAMUEL PEPYS
By D. Le Marchand

Family worship is a regular practice in the household, so much so that on several occasions the master regrets that his return home in a slightly intoxicated condition makes it expedient to violate the custom, for fear of infringing due decorum, an omission which causes some scandal.[77] All this is perfunctory. But when the great catastrophe of Deb. Willet comes, we have seen that the distress of it drives Pepys to his knees: "I did this night promise to my wife never to go to bed without calling upon God upon my knees by prayer, and I begun this night, and hope I shall never forget to do the like all my life; for I do find that it is much the best for my soul and body to live pleasing to God and my poor wife, and will ease me of much care as well as much expense." [78]

Always shrewd, you see, always practical, always with a canny, careful instinct for the saving of expense, even in matters of God. God was a universal institution to turn to when you wanted something. He was an obscure, terrible, overmastering institution, which blasted you and blighted you, when, as so often, you did those things which you ought not: "It is a cold, which God Almighty in justice did give me while I sat lewdly sporting with Mrs. Lane the other day with the broken window in my neck." [79] It may seem strange that God should bother with the fantastic tricks of such petty creatures, but he does, and we should bear ourselves conformably — if we could.

So much for the dire hours of need and terror. But in general it cannot be said that Pepys was spiritually obsessed by the essentials of religion. God is frequently and reverently mentioned in the Diary. He is mentioned still more frequently in the later correspondence, and the testimony as to Pepys's dying moments shows that he passed away decorously as a good Christian should. But through the Diary, at any rate, considering the general frankness in treating all subjects, there is singularly little reference to a future life, though the writer, of course, took it for granted. There is no suggestion whatever of the abiding, haunting sense of God, longing for God, thirst for God, which inspire every page of Amiel, or of the "Imitation." Pepys simply knew nothing about these matters. He was a healthy, practical man of the world, largely and constantly occupied with getting and spending, eating and drinking, loving and hating, and music. God belonged to church and Sunday and your best clothes and ministers and death and heaven, all things to be treated with immense respect and to be avoided and postponed as much as possible, while you hurried to do what had to be done here.

Perhaps it will be thought that, in discussing a

238

busy, active, external, material life, I am giving too much weight to God altogether. It is because the vast, brooding consciousness of God alone gives such a life all its significance — and all its emptiness, and because I believe the busy, active, external, material life of America to-day, so much the life personified by the great Diarist, needs God more than anything else to save it. How the need is to be satisfied is another question, and one that can never be answered from the Diary of Pepys.

THE END

NOTES

List of the most important works referred to, with the abbreviations used.

The Diary of Samuel Pepys, M.A., F.R.S., edited, with additions, by Henry B. Wheatley, 9 volumes, 1893–1901.   *Diary.*

The Diary and Correspondence of Samuel Pepys, edited by Rev. Mynors Bright, 6 volumes.   Bright.

The Life, Journals, and Correspondence of Samuel Pepys, edited by Rev. John Smith, 2 volumes.   Smith.

Wheatley, Henry B., *Samuel Pepys and the World He Lived In.*   Wheatley.

Moorhouse, E. H., *Samuel Pepys, Administrator, Observer, Gossip.*   Moorhouse.

I. THE MAN AND THE DIARY

1. Printed only in Smith.
2. *History of England*, vol. I, chap. III.
3. Moorhouse, p. 302.
4. Berkeley to Pepys, February 23, 1668, Bright, vol. VI, p. 121.
5. *Diary*, vol. I, p. xvi.
6. *Diary*, November 1, 1660, vol. I, p. 253.
7. Evelyn's *Diary*, May 26, 1703.
8. *Diary*, vol. I, p. xlv.
9. Epigraph of *Journal.*
10. *Journal des Goncourts*, February 19, 1869, vol. III, p. 271.
11. *Journal des Goncourts*, March 6, 1882, vol. VI, p. 185.
12. Maine de Biran, *Sa Vie et Ses Pensées*, p. 128.
13. *Journal*, vol. I, p. 393.
14. *Memoirs of John Quincy Adams*, vol. II, p. 148.
15. *Diary*, vol. I, p. 1.
16. Wheatley, p. 16.
17. *Diary*, June 13, 1667, vol. VI, p. 342.
18. *Diary*, March 9, 1669, vol. VIII, p. 239.
19. *Mémoires du Duc de Saint-Simon*, edition Hachette, 1884, vol. V, p. 429.
20. *Diary*, September 30, 1661, vol. II, p. 105.

NOTES

41. *Diary*, April 9, 1661, vol. ii, p. 5.
42. *Diary*, January 12, 1661, vol. i, p. 301.
43. *Diary*, November 24, 1665, vol. v, p. 144.
44. *Diary*, August 9, 1662, vol. ii, p. 284.
45. *Diary*, June 6, 1667, vol. vi, p. 332.
46. *Diary*, October 23, 1667, vol. vii, p. 157.
47. *Diary*, May 8, 1662, vol. ii, p. 218.
48. *Diary*, March 7, 1666, vol. v, p. 227.
49. *Diary*, December 15, 1663, vol. iii, p. 356.
50. *Diary*, June 25, 1665, vol. iv, p. 420.
51. *Diary*, February 7, 1665, vol. iv, p. 328.
52. *Diary*, January 21, 1665, vol. iv, p. 316.
53. *Diary*, March 21, 1663, vol. iii, p. 68.
54. *Diary*, March 22, 1663, vol. iii, p. 69.
55. *Diary*, May 21, 1667, vol. vi, p. 309.
56. *Diary*, February 21, 1667, vol. vi, p. 180.
57. *Diary*, August 22, 1666, vol. v, p. 384.
58. *Diary*, April 5, 1667, vol. vi, p. 245.
59. *Diary*, July 30, 1667, vol. vii, p. 49.
60. *Diary*, vol. ix, p. 235.
61. My attention was called to this pamphlet by Mr. A. C. Potter.
62. Moorhouse, p. 46, *Diary*, vol. ix, p. 236.
63. *Diary*, May 29, 1667, vol. vi, p. 323.
64. *Diary*, June 13, 1663, vol. iii, p. 156.
65. To Berkeley, February 22, 1678, Bright, vol. vi, p. 120.
66. *Diary*, May 12, 1665, vol. iv, p. 384.
67. To Thomas Pepys, February 1, 1679, Bright, vol. vi, p. 123.
68. *Diary*, February 19, 1669, vol. viii, p. 220.
69. *Diary*, June 15, 1667, vol. vi, p. 351.
70. *Diary*, December 19, 1663, vol. iii, p. 358.
71. *Diary*, April 12, 1665, vol. iv, p. 367.
72. *Diary*, October 30, 1662, vol. ii, p. 357.
73. *Diary*, August 23, 1668, vol. viii, p. 82.
74. *Diary*, June 27, 1667, vol. vi, p. 372.
75. *Diary*, October 27, 1665, vol. v, p. 121.
76. *Diary*, March 4, 1668, vol. vii, p. 326.
77. *Diary*, March 6, 1668, vol. vii, p. 329.

NOTES

III. PEPYS AND HIS MONEY

1. *Diary*, August 20, 1663, vol. III, p. 240.
2. *Diary*, July 9, 1667, vol. VII, p. 13.
3. *Diary*, September 30, 1662, vol. II, p. 328.
4. *Diary*, January 1, 1665, vol. IV, p. 301.
5. *Diary*, September 22, 1667, vol. VII, p. 112.
6. *Diary*, July 13, 1661, vol. II, p. 61.
7. *Diary*, November 9, 1667, vol. VII, p. 178.
8. *Diary*, vol. I, p. 3.
9. *Diary*, January 29, 1660, vol. I, p. 34.
10. *Diary*, May 30, 1660, vol. I, p. 155.
11. *Diary*, July 7, 1660, vol. I, p. 180.
12. *Diary*, January 25, 1664, vol. IV, p. 21.
13. *Diary*, September 14, 1664, vol. IV, p. 227.
14. *Diary*, September 16, 1664, vol. IV, p. 227.
15. *Diary*, April 27, 1664, vol. IV, 113.
16. *Diary*, September 29, 1662, vol. II, p. 326.
17. *Diary*, January 2, 1668, vol. VII, p. 249.
18. *Diary*, February 2, 1664, vol. IV, p. 29.
19. *Diary*, May 18, 1664, vol. IV, p. 128.
20. *Diary*, July 21, 1664, vol. IV, p. 181.
21. *Diary*, December 31, 1661, vol. II, p. 152.
22. *Diary*, May 1, 1663, vol. III, p. 100.
23. *Diary*, July 6, 1661, vol. II, p. 60.
24. *Diary*, January 15, 1664, vol. IV, p. 13.
25. *Diary*, October 13, 1662, vol. II, p. 338.
26. *Diary*, November 24, 1662, vol. II, p. 375.
27. *Diary*, September 16, 1663, vol. III, p. 262.
28. *Diary*, June 27, 1661, vol. II, p. 56.
29. *Diary*, September 21, 1664, vol. IV, p. 231.
30. *Diary*, December 31, 1667, vol. VI, p. 112.
31. *Diary*, March 2, 1662, vol. II, p. 186.
32. *Diary*, August 18, 1664, vol. IV, p. 206.
33. *Diary*, September 12, 1664, vol. IV, p. 226.
34. *Diary*, January 1, 1668, vol. VII, p. 246.
35. *Diary*, June 30, 1666, vol. V, p. 328.
36. *Diary*, January 30, 1665, vol. IV, p. 322.
37. *Diary*, October 10, 1667, vol. VII, p. 135.

NOTES

38. *Diary*, October 7, 1666, vol. VI, p. 10.
39. *Diary*, October 17, 1666, vol. VI, p. 23.
40. *Diary*, February 7, 1667, vol. VI, p. 157.
41. *Diary*, February 8, 1667, vol. VI, p. 157.
42. *Diary*, October 14, 1662, vol. II, p. 339.
43. *Diary*, January 24, 1660, vol. I, p. 29.
44. *Diary*, November 12, 1660, vol. I, p. 261.
45. *Diary*, January 2, 1661, vol. I, p. 293.
46. *Diary*, October 10, 1667, vol. VII, p. 134.
47. *Diary*, October 11, 1667, vol. VII, p. 137.
48. *Diary*, September 1, 1663, vol. III, p. 249.
49. *Diary*, September 12, 1665, vol. V, p. 70.
50. *Diary*, March 25, 1666, vol. V, p. 239.
51. *Diary*, June 10, 1668, vol. VIII, p. 39.
52. *Diary*, November 29, 1667, vol. VII, p. 204.
53. *Diary*, July 11, 1664, vol. IV, p. 168.
54. *Diary*, April 18, 1661, vol. II, p. 13.
55. *Diary*, September 18, 1665, vol. V, p. 79.
56. *Diary*, October 20, 1663, vol. III, p. 289.
57. *"A King and No King,"* by Beaumont and Fletcher, Act II, scene 2.
58. *Diary*, May 28, 1667, vol. VI, p. 322.
59. *Diary*, July 14, 1664, vol. IV, p. 172.
60. *Diary*, January 29, 1666, vol. V, p. 198.
61. *Diary*, July 24, 1661, vol. II, p. 65.
62. *Diary*, January 20, 1664, vol. IV, p. 18.
63. *Diary*, January 11, 1664, vol. IV, p. 10.
64. H. Wanley to Dr. Charlett, March 8, 1701, Bright, vol. VI, p. 233.
65. *Diary*, January 2, 1662, vol. II, p. 153.
66. *Diary*, January 7, 1664, vol. IV, p. 6.
67. *Diary*, November 16, 1662, vol. II, p. 370.
68. *Diary*, August 3, 1660, vol. I, p. 198.
69. *Diary*, June 14, 1664, vol. IV, p. 149.
70. *Diary*, July 24, 1665, vol. V, p. 22.
71. *Diary*, May 22, 1662, vol. II, p. 226.
72. *Diary*, October 17, 1667, vol. VII, p. 144.
73. *Diary*, September 14, 1662, vol. II, p. 317.
74. *Diary*, November 9, 1665, vol. V, p. 133.

NOTES

75. *Diary*, December 17, 1665, vol. v, p. 164.
76. *Diary*, July 14, 1662, vol. ii, p. 264.
77. *Diary*, December 20, 1663, vol. iii, p. 359.
78. *Diary*, December 28, 1664, vol. iv, p. 297.
79. *Diary*, February 14, 1660, vol. i, p. 54.
80. *Diary*, February 17, 1662, vol. ii, p. 178.
81. *Diary*, January 13, 1662, vol. ii, p. 160.
82. *Diary*, March 4, 1669, vol. viii, p. 233.
83. *Diary*, April 11, 1661, vol. ii, p. 8.
84. *Diary*, August 14, 1666, vol. v, p. 375.
85. *Diary*, November 11, 1661, vol. ii, p. 127.
86. *Diary*, March 6, 1660, vol. i, p. 76.
87. *Diary*, March 27, 1661, vol. i, p. 340.
88. *Diary*, January 6, 1668, vol. vii, p. 254.
89. *Diary*, March 2, 1669, vol. viii, p. 227.

V. PEPYS AND HIS INTELLECT

1. *Diary*, March 26, 1666, vol. v, p. 240.
2. *Diary*, August 8, 1662, vol. ii, p. 282.
3. *Diary*, October 15, 1666, vol. vi, p. 22.
4. *Diary*, March 27, 1665, vol. iv, p. 358.
5. *Diary*, January 15, 1665, vol. iv, p. 311.
6. *Diary*, November 3, 1661, vol. ii, p. 122.
7. *Diary*, February 23, 1668, vol. viii, p. 222.
8. *Diary*, July 25, 1664, vol. iv, p. 186.
9. *Diary*, July 4, 1662, vol. ii, p. 259.
10. *Diary*, December 23, 1664, vol. iv, p. 294.
11. *Diary*, August 19, 1665, vol. v, p. 49.
12. *Diary*, August 8, 1666, vol. v, p. 370.
13. *Diary*, July 10, 1667, vol. vi, p. 338.
14. *Diary*, April 28, 1667, vol. vi, p. 276.
15. *Diary*, August 19, 1666, vol. v, p. 382.
16. *Diary*, February 15, 1665, vol. iv, p. 331.
17. *Diary*, March 1, 1665, vol. iv, p. 341.
18. *Diary*, February 15, 1665, vol. iv, p. 332.
19. Newton to Pepys, November 26, 1693, Bright, vol. vi, p. 177.
20. *Diary*, January 27, 1664, vol. iv, p. 22.

NOTES

VI. PEPYS AND HIS WIFE

1. See *Blackwood's Magazine*, vol. CCIX; also E. Barrington, *The Ladies.*
2. *Diary*, vol. I, p. XXVII.
3. *Diary*, November 13, 1662, vol. II, p. 368.
4. *Diary*, January 9, 1663, vol. III, pp. 9, 10.
5. *Diary*, February 15, 1663, vol. III, p. 38.
6. *Diary*, January 6, 1664, vol. IV, p. 5.
7. *Diary*, February 4, 1667, vol. VI, p. 153.
8. *Diary*, May 29, 1667, vol. VI, p. 323.
9. *Diary*, vol. I, p. XVIII.
10. *Diary*, October 25, 1668, vol. VIII, p. 123.
11. *Diary*, December 6, 1668, vol. VIII, p. 163.
12. *Diary*, February 27, 1668, vol. VII, p. 320.
13. *Diary*, February 25, 1667, vol. VI, p. 185.
14. *Diary*, December 25, 1665, vol. V, p. 171.
15. *Diary*, vol. I, p. XVIII.
16. Thomas Moore, *Memoirs, Correspondence, and Diary,* August 29, 1822, vol. III, p. 367.
17. *Diary*, July 26, 1664, vol. IV, p. 186.
18. *Diary*, September 22, 1664, vol. IV, p. 233.
19. *Diary*, May 12, 1669, vol. VIII, p. 303.
20. *Diary*, vol. I, p. XXVII.
21. *Diary*, June 7, 1663, vol. III, p. 152.
22. *Diary*, September 10, 1668, vol. VIII, p. 96.
23. *Diary*, May 4, 1666, vol. V, p. 268.
24. *Diary*, May 2, 1663, vol. III, p. 102.
25. *Diary*, July 12, 1667, vol. VII, p. 18.
26. *Diary*, June 17, 1668, vol. VIII, p. 48.
27. *Diary*, August 7, 1665, vol. V, p. 38.
28. *Diary*, May 12, 1666, vol. V, p. 272.
29. *Diary*, February 4, 1665, vol. IV, p. 327.
30. Wheatley, p. 44.
31. *Diary*, March 14, 1664, vol. IV, p. 69.
32. *Diary*, August 13, 1663, vol. III, p. 234.
33. *Diary*, February 21, 1665, vol. IV, p. 335.
34. *Diary*, May 11, 1667, vol. VI, p. 296.
35. *Diary*, December 21, 1668, vol. VIII, p. 174.
36. *Diary*, Ibid.

NOTES

37. *Diary*, Ibid.
38. *Diary*, May 26, 1663, vol. III, p. 134.
39. *Diary*, January 2, 1665, vol. IV, p. 303.
40. *Diary*, November 2, 1662, vol. II, p. 360.
41. *Diary*, December 27, 1663, vol. III, p. 366.
42. *Diary*, September 13, 1663, vol. III, p. 260.
43. *Diary*, June 15, 1663, vol. III, p. 160.
44. *Diary*, February 15, 1668, vol. VII, p. 301.
45. *Diary*, November 17, 1663, vol. III, p. 325.
46. *Diary*, September 14, 1663, vol. III, p. 261.
47. *Diary*, June 21, 1668, vol. VIII, p. 51.
48. *Diary*, February 26, 1664, vol. IV, p. 53.
49. *Diary*, March 5, 1668, vol. VII, p. 326.
50. *Diary*, September 6, 1664, vol. IV, p. 221.
51. *Diary*, May 23, 1667, vol. VI, p. 316.
52. *Diary*, March 19, 1667, vol. VI, p. 217.
53. *The Private Journal of Aaron Burr*, edited by William K. Bixby, September 5, 1809, vol. II, p. 228.
54. *Diary*, February 11, 1667, vol. VI, p. 161.
55. *Diary*, November 11, 1668, vol. VIII, p. 140.
56. *Diary*, vol. VIII, pp. 149, 158.
57. *Diary*, November 19, 1668, vol. VIII, p. 149.
58. Sir Frederick Bridge, *Samuel Pepys, Lover of Musique*, p. 115.
59. Pepys to James Houblon, July 10, 1689, Smith, vol. II, p. 219.

VII. PEPYS AND GOD

1. *Diary*, March 4, 1660, vol. I, p. 74.
2. *Diary*, November 1, 1660, vol. I, p. 253.
3. *Diary*, July 18, 1668, vol. VIII, p. 64.
4. *Diary*, September 4, 1668, vol. VIII, p. 92.
5. *Diary*, February, 18, 1666, vol. V, p. 212.
6. *Diary*, January 23, 1667, vol. VI, p. 136.
7. Ibid.
8. Ibid.
9. *Diary*, December 24, 1667, vol. VII, p. 232.
10. Ibid.

NOTES

11. *Diary*, April 10, 1661, vol. II, p. 6.
12. *Diary*, April 17, 1664, vol. IV, p. 104.
13. *Diary*, November 8, 1663, vol. III, p. 312.
14. *Diary*, October 6, 1661, vol. II, p. 110.
15. *Diary*, September 9, 1666, vol. V, p. 407.
16. *Diary*, June 17, 1666, vol. V, p. 311.
17. *Diary*, August 3, 1662, vol. II, p. 278.
18. *Diary*, October 26, 1662, vol. II, p. 351.
19. *Diary*, October 2, 1664, vol. IV, p. 240.
20. *Diary*, October 9, 1664, vol. IV, p. 245.
21. *Diary*, August 18, 1667, vol. VII, p. 67.
22. *Diary*, May 12, 1661, vol. II, p. 32.
23. *Diary*, April 23, 1665, vol. IV, p. 374.
24. *Diary*, July 8, 1660, vol. I, p. 181.
25. *Diary*, April 7, 1662, vol. II, p. 203.
26. *Diary*, January 31, 1668, vol. VII, p. 280.
27. *Diary*, August 9, 1663, vol. III, p. 227.
28. *Diary*, January 21, 1660, vol. I, p. 26.
29. *Diary*, February 16, 1662, vol. II, p. 178.
30. *Diary*, February 10, 1667, vol. VI, p. 158.
31. *Diary*, May 19, 1667, vol. VI, p. 307.
32. *Diary*, April 3, 1667, vol. VI, p. 238.
33. *Diary*, November 24, 1661, vol. II, p. 133.
34. *Diary*, November 25, 1666, vol. VI, p. 73.
35. *Diary*, May 24, 1668, vol. VIII, p. 26.
36. *Diary*, August 23, 1668, vol. VIII, p. 81.
37. *Diary*, August 25, 1661, vol. II, p. 82.
38. *Diary*, January 19, 1662, vol. II, p. 163.
39. *Diary*, November 30, 1662, vol. II, p. 380.
40. *Diary*, May 27, 1668, vol. VIII, p. 30.
41. *Diary*, February 15, 1660, vol. I, p. 55.
42. *Diary*, September 6, 1668, vol. VIII, p. 93.
43. *Diary*, June 12, 1661, vol. II, p. 50.
44. *Diary*, February 17, 1667, vol. VI, p. 172.
45. *Diary*, April 5, 1667, vol. VI, p. 244.
46. *Diary*, May 15, 1660, vol. I, p. 132.
47. *Diary*, October 2, 1660, vol. I, p. 234.
48. *Diary*, May 8, 1663, vol. III, p. 107.
49. *Diary*, November 24, 1666, vol. VI, p. 72.

NOTES

50. *Diary*, June 14, 1667, vol. VI, p. 348.
51. See in Bright, vol. VI various letters to and from Lord Reay.
52. April 23, 1661, vol. II, p. 22.
53. *Diary*, June 15, 1663, vol. III, p. 160.
54. *Tangier Journal*, September 11, 1683, Smith, vol. I, p. 353.
55. *Diary*, March 23, 1669, vol. VIII, p. 256.
56. *Anatomy of Melancholy*, Part 2, section 5, member 1, sub-section 5.
57. *Diary*, September 3, 1661, vol. II, p. 90.
58. *Diary*, December 31, 1664, vol. IV, p. 300.
59. *Diary*, January 20, 1665, vol. IV, p. 315.
60. *Diary*, March 26, 1664, vol. IV, p. 357.
61. In Sainte-Beuve, *Portraits Littéraires*, vol. III, p. 251.
62. *Diary*, January 4, 1664, vol. IV, p. 4.
63. *Diary*, January 2, 1664, vol. IV, p. 2.
64. *Diary*, February 3, 1665, vol. IV, p. 325.
65. *Diary*, October 31, 1662, vol. II, p. 358.
66. *Diary*, December 26, 1662, vol. II, p. 399.
67. *Diary*, May 20, 1667, vol. VI, p. 308.
68. *Diary*, March 26, 1667, vol. VI, p. 226.
69. *Diary*, August 8, 1664, vol. IV, p. 197.
70. *Diary*, July 26, 1661, vol. II, p. 67.
71. *Diary*, October 21, 1661, vol. II, p. 116.
72. *Diary*, September 9, 1662, vol. II, p. 313, also January 17, 1663, vol. III, p. 15.
73. *Diary*, October 20, 1662, vol. II, p. 346.
74. *Diary*, January 30, 1667, vol. VI, p. 145.
75. *Diary*, December 12, 1663, vol. III, p. 351.
76. *Diary*, May 30, 1663, vol. III, p. 141.
77. *Diary*, September 29, 1661, vol. II, p. 103, also November 10, 1661, vol. II, p. 126.
78. *Diary*, November 20, 1668, vol. VIII, p. 151.
79. *Diary*, September 27, 1663, vol. III, p. 271.

INDEX

studious to learn all necessary things, 43; of a worrying temperament, 44, 73, 74, 75; his health, 45, 46; cut for the stone, 45, 46; had the instinct of order, 46, 47; his attitude with his superiors, 48–51; believed in discipline, 52; had the faculty of working with others, 56, 57; adroit in keeping out of quarrels, 59, 60; his honesty, 61, 62, 76; as to bribes or presents, 62, 63, 76–79; had a human instinct of money-getting, 64, 71; normally ambitious, 64, 65; a real patriot, 66, 67; great speech in Parliament, 68, 69; characteristics, 70 n.

Believed in keeping systematic, exact accounts, 72, 73, 189; sources of his money, 75–82; inheritances, 80–82; saving, 83, 84; investing, 85, 86; spending, 88–99; the great matter of clothes, 89, 90; amusements, 90, 91; had a passion for books, 92, 93, 148; domestic outlay, 93–96; gets a coach, 97, 98; the needs of his relatives, 99–101; and of his wife's relatives, 101, 102; charity, 102, 103; did not leave a large property, 104.

Watched men live, 105; London his normal atmosphere, 106, 154; seldom makes the reader laugh with him, 106, 107; a practical joker, 107, 108; sensitive to human sorrow, 108, 109; considerate of animals, 110; believed in family discipline, 111, 112; relations with his mother, 113–15; with his father, 116, 117; with his brothers and sister, 117-21; with his wife's relatives, 122; average in courage, 123–25; not closely intimate with any one, 126; attitude to his social superiors, 126–28; liked good company, 128, 129; and good women, 130, 131; had social handicaps, 131–34; games and sports, 134, 135; merry

journeys, 135, 136; dancing, 136–38; as a host, 137–39.

Had a normally clear and vigorous intellect, 140; somewhat cynical, 141; never hesitates to commend himself, 142; his intellectual powers well trained, 144; interested in scientific matters, 145, 146, 148; president of the Royal Society, 147; an author, 149; his reading, 150; not a great lover of poetry, 151; met most of the literary men of his time, 151, 152; his opinions in literature, 152; bored by *Hudibras*, 153; greatly interested in painting, 155–57; enjoyed the theatre, 159–62; was familiar with actors and dramatists, 162; his opinions of plays, 163–65; enjoyed and appreciated music, 165–68, 174, 175; composed songs, 168; tried to teach Mrs. Pepys, 169; and some of the maids, 170; a musical critic, 171, 172; cared little for religious music, 173.

Relations with his wife, 176–209; quarrels with her, 179, 186–89, 193; his affection for her, 183, 193, 194, 197–99; shows lack of conjugal sentiment, 184, 185; critical of domestic management, 191; jealous, 195, 196; sensitive to feminine charm, 200, 201; not vain about his amours, 202; the Diary reeks with love-affairs, 203; foreign gibberish used in recording them, 204, 236; the affair of Deb. Willet, 205–08, 237.

A loyal member of the Church of England, 210; his respect for the Puritans, 210, 211; some contacts with Catholicism, 211–13; a faithful church-goer, 213; but often distracted from the service, 214–17; comments on preachers, 217–22; fond of theological discussion, 222–24; fearfully interested in ghosts and apparitions, 225, 226; super-

INDEX

stition and magic, 226, 227; addicted to making vows, 227-34; conscience always at his elbow, 234, 235; as to prayer and the need of God, 236–39.

Pepys, Mrs. Samuel, 7, 8, 79, 95, 120, 150, 160, 232; not a careful spender, 98, 99; her relatives, 101, 102, 122; did not get on well with her husband's kin, 121, 122; her face and her voice, 169, 170, 192; imaginary diary of, 177; a child of fifteen when married, 177, 191; intensely social, 177, 178; but rather solitary, 178, 179; had no children, 179, 185, 186; her diversions, 179, 180; her taste in dress, 180, 181; her religion, 181, 182; her feeling toward her husband, 182-84, 195, 205-08; quarrels with him, 179, 186-90; paints charmingly, 188, 189; as a housewife, 192; had her faults, 195; illness, 198, 199; death, 208, 209.

Pepys, Thomas, 80, 101, 117, 118.
Pepysian Library, the, 70 n., 92.
Peters, Lady, 26.
Pett, Commissioner, 56, 214.
Petty, Sir William, 148.
Plague, the, in London, 30, 41.
Polyglot modesty, 204.
Ponsonby, Arthur, 11 n.
Popish Plot, the, 6, 213.
Porter, Sir Joseph, 37.
Portugal, Queen of, 23.
Povy, Thomas, 25, 26, 58, 141.
Preachers, curious and entertaining, 217–20.
Puritans, influence of, 1, 2, 3, 26, 158, 159; Pepys's respect for, 210, 211.

Recorder, the, Pepys's admiration of, 167.
Reeves, Mr., 146, 147.
Restoration period, the, 1, 2, 21, 26, 27.
Rickard, Sir Andrew, 62.
Royal Society, the, 147.

Rupert, Prince, 50, 51, 142.

Saint-Simon, Duc de, Memoirs of, 11, 15, 21, 22, 30.
Sainte-Beuve, Charles Augustin, 16.
St. Michel, Elizabeth (Mrs. Samuel Pepys), 7, 8.
Sands, Mr., 68.
Sandwich, Lord, 5, 86, 127, 128, 200, 223.
Saving, the habit of, 83, 84.
Scott, Sir Walter, 40.
Selden, John, 42.
Self-expression, instinct of, 12, 20.
Servants, 95, 96, 111, 112, 170, 191.
Sewall, Samuel, 19.
Shadwell, Thomas, 162.
Shakespeare, William, 32, 150, 228; and the Baconians, 158; Pepys's comments on, 164.
Sheres, Sir Henry, 98.
Sidney, Sir Philip, 196.
Sisyphus, 234, 236.
Snorers, 107.
Sobriety of grief, 191, 192.
Social handicaps, the greatest of all, 132.
Spending, the habit of, 83, 84.
Spong, Mr., 53.
Stankes, William, 22.
Sterne, Laurence, on the cant of criticism, 153.
Stillingfleet, Edward, 218.
Stuarts, restoration of the, 1, 2, 3, 26, 27, 28, 38.

Talking things over, comfort in, 57.
Tangier, 5, 77, 78, 105, 154.
Tanner, J. R., 70 n.
Tar, buying, 63, 78.
Tax returns, the eternal torment of, 61.
Teaching, better formerly than now, 144.
Teddiman, Sir Thomas, 24, 25.
Theatre, the, 29, 90; in the Renaissance period, 157; an epitome of life,

261

INDEX